Judo Unleashed

Judo Unleashed

Neil Ohlenkamp

McGraw·Hill

New York   Chicago   San Francisco   Lisbon   London   Madrid   Mexico City
Milan   New Delhi   San Juan   Seoul   Singapore   Sydney   Toronto

First McGraw-Hill edition, 2006.

6 7 8 9 0001090/Ref # : KKDN 01780/2639 0

ISBN: 0-07-147534-6

The Library of Congress Cataloging-in-Publication Data is available on file.

DISCLAIMER

Judo involves moves that can cause serious injury. Although the author
and publisher have made every effort to ensure that the information in this
book was accurate at the time of going to press, they accept no liability
for loss, accident, injury, or inconvenience sustained by anyone using this
book or following the advice given in it. The techniques in this book
should always be practiced under the direct supervision of
a qualified black belt judo instructor.

McGraw-Hill books are available at special quantity discounts to use as
premiums and sales promotions, or for use in corporate training programs.
For more information, please write to the Director of Special Sales,
Professional Publishing, McGraw-Hill, Two Penn Plaza, New York, NY
10121-2298. Or contact your local bookseller.

Printed in and bound in Malaysia.

Contents

Using this book

This book is a manual of the main principles and techniques of Kodokan judo. The Kodokan is the original school of judo in Tokyo, Japan, founded in 1882. The techniques in the standard syllabus of judo are included as a reference, but there are many variations of each technique. The photographs in this book demonstrate the basic positions of the techniques and some variations, but they are by no means comprehensive.

Participating in a judo class with other students and a qualified judo instructor is the only way to develop skill in judo. This book is intended to give readers a greater understanding of judo, and to be a study aid and reference for students up to the level of black belt, but its limited size prohibits more detailed explanations or additional advanced techniques. Be assured that there is much more to learning judo than what is included here, just as the black belt level is only the beginning step in learning judo.

The technique names, Japanese terminology, and English translations used in these chapters are those used in the official *Kodokan New Japanese-English Dictionary of Judo* (Kodokan Judo Institute, 2000) and *Kodokan Judo* by Jigoro Kano (Kodansha International, 1994). Other names and terms may be used in various judo schools around the world, but these are believed to be the most widely accepted.

DEDICATION

This book is dedicated to all judo teachers who share their knowledge and love of judo with their students, and specifically to *Sensei* Juergen Wahl, who has been an example and guide to me for nearly four decades.

To teach is to touch an unknown number of lives, even in future generations. As Henry Adams once said, "A teacher affects eternity; he can never tell where his influence stops."

Let's begin (*hajime!*)

Skill in judo can only be attained on the mat, working with partners in an organized training program under the guidance of an expert judo instructor, or *sensei*, which literally means "one who has gone before." A *sensei* has been in your position and learned the lessons you seek. By providing a good example and demonstrating proper technique, a *sensei* helps you understand the techniques and acts as a model by which to gauge your own performance.

You also learn from everyone with whom you practice, so seek instruction from a wide variety of people. You will soon see that even the model technique performed by your *sensei* may need to be modified to take advantage of your own strengths, weaknesses, body type, or speed. Likewise, the technique may vary depending on your opponent's height, weight, movement, or abilities. Knowing this, you should feel free to try different methods after learning the basic principle of a throw or grappling technique.

This book is designed to give you ideas for techniques, variations, and methods not seen in class. Like practicing with a new *sensei*, it may expose you to fresh ideas, or reinforce the basic principles.

In either case, it will supplement your training by helping you to visualize the techniques and understand the key points that make judo work with minimal effort.

Which is the best martial art? The one you will enjoy practicing for the rest of your life.

Understanding judo theory

A palpable understanding of most judo principles comes only through hard physical training, but these chapters aim to provide glimpses of the underlying theories that explain how the physical moves work, and to explore larger fighting principles that can be learned in judo. These are seldom discussed in depth during class, but your performance will improve as you deepen your understanding of the judo theory and concepts covered in this book. Recognizing the limitless nature of attacks, you would have to learn an infinite number of techniques to master every potential situation. If you strive to understand the principles behind the art of attack and defense, you should learn to respond more intuitively and naturally—even to new situations.

One objective of this manual is to help you through rough spots in training by motivating and encouraging you to see the possibilities as you prepare for each new rank. It cannot replace self-discipline, but it can act as a reference to show you the light at the end of the tunnel. To earn a black belt, you must devote a considerable part of your life to judo so you should know in advance that it is achievable and worth it.

Is judo a sport or martial art?

Judo is many things to different people. It is a sport, an art, a discipline, a recreational activity, a fitness programme, a study of Japanese culture, a means of self-defence, and a way of life. It is both one of the most popular sports and the most widely practiced martial art in the world.

CLASSICAL JUDO

Judo is a refinement of the combat systems of older Japanese *jujutsu*, where mastery of the art was essential to a warrior's survival in battle. Jigoro Kano, the founder of judo, was born in 1860 and studied traditional styles of *jujutsu* during his youth, when all martial arts were beginning to die out. While mastering the *Kito Ryu* and *Tenjinshinyo Ryu* styles of *jujutsu* he became devoted to teaching and preserving the older ways of fighting.

He sought to retain much of the traditional Japanese culture and fighting methods in judo, partly by emphasizing the value of the continued practice of dangerous combat techniques, including various strikes to sensitive areas and defenses against weapons.

For this he promoted the use of a rehearsed training method called *kata*. He recognized that certain techniques and practice methods were in danger of disappearing because changing times meant they were no longer needed by the warrior class. By updating the practice of judo to make it more safe, effective, and relevant for modern society, he saved much of the ancient warriors' knowledge and passed it on to new generations.

Jigoro Kano was both a traditionalist and an innovator. Although concerned about the loss of tradition during Japan's modernization, he embraced many changes. In 1882 he founded the Kodokan as the original school of judo—the first Japanese martial art of the modern era. It successfully preserved the techniques and spirit of *jujutsu* while at the same time breaking away from some of its traditional practice methods. Changes were made to ensure participants' safety, improve effectiveness, and emphasize certain overall principles.

The refinements began by identifying the most dangerous moves of judo, and restricting these to *kata* practice. This permitted Jigoro Kano to improve on *jujutsu* training methods by focusing on the use of real-life free practice, or *randori*, with techniques that could be applied safely with full force against an opponent. It was a major advance in martial arts training, greatly improving the effectiveness of judo compared to earlier martial arts.

The development of *randori* as a form of practice led to a safe way to test and improve physical skills and combat spirit via competition, or *shiai*. Jigoro Kano created the first annual Red and White Tournament at the Kodokan in

The many facets of Judo

Judo is more about self-discovery than memorization of moves. Like a fine diamond, it has many facets reflecting the light of the world around it; each time you look at judo, another reveals its brilliance.

- Judo can be applied without injuring an opponent, but it has also saved the lives of many students faced with real attacks.
- Judo has consistently proven its effectiveness in a wide range of tests, from ancient *jujutsu* contests to modern mixed martial arts matches.
- Judo is included in military hand-to-hand combat training to efficiently apply force in a deadly manner.
- Judo competition is enjoyed by young children at local tournaments, and by elite male and female athletes who represent their countries at the Olympic Games, performing awesome feats of skill.
- Judo principles are studied in the best business schools around the world to help corporate leaders use power properly, utilize leverage, and apply it in the right direction, as well as take advantage of competitors' greater strength and size by using it against them.
- Verbal judo is taught in many law enforcement agencies to provide officers with methods to de-escalate and control dangerous situations without using force.
- Judo is based on sound principles that help students develop character and become experts at dealing with all kinds of conflicts in life.

1884. This competition continues today as one of the longest-running sporting events in the world, predating the modern Olympics by 12 years. The Kodokan also held the first All-Japan Judo Championships in 1930.

As other modern sports began to form and judo was introduced into the public school system as a form of physical education, judo gradually developed a competitive sport element that helped to popularize it as a physical education system for the masses around the world.

As principal of the first teachers' training university in Tokyo, Jigoro Kano led Japan through great educational reform, and was the first Japanese delegate to the International Olympic Committee. Considered the father of sport in Japan, he oversaw and encouraged significant evolution of judo during his lifetime. Sometimes called *Kano-ryu jujutsu* early on, judo eventually overshadowed *jujutsu*, which all but disappeared for nearly 100 years as many of its styles merged into judo. Much of judo's popularity in Japan was a result of proven success in competitions, such as the great tournament of 1886 where the Kodokan defeated the feared *jujutsu* masters of the Meiji era.

Based on experience in competition, judo continued to change and adapt its techniques. One famous tournament against *Fusen-ryu jujutsu* masters around the turn of the 20th century revealed a weakness in the judo syllabus and resulted in strengthening judo matwork by incorporating some *Fusen-ryu* techniques and training methods.

Jigoro Kano was always looking for ways to improve the performance of judo students in contest. Based on tournament results, some techniques were banned because they were too dangerous, while new techniques were adopted once they proved effective. He recognized it was not only the type of techniques that determined the success or failure of a competitor or fighter; by focussing on training methods, he revolutionized the classical *jujutsu* approach to training. Counterintuitive as it seems, by separating the most dangerous techniques from free practice, he created a training method that actually permitted students to become more dangerous as fighters.

Martial artists soon discovered that only by regular *randori* and *shiai* against fully resisting opponents did they gain the necessary skills to apply the techniques in a real situation—something not possible by practicing lightly against co-operating partners. Jigoro Kano realized that the most successful training results in body and mind working together instinctively to respond to unique situations with accuracy and confidence, rather than with theoretical, predetermined, or tentative actions.

EVOLUTION OF SPORT JUDO

After Jigoro Kano's death in 1938—followed closely by World War II, the occupation of Japan, and the westernization of Japanese culture—judo went through a period of turmoil. It was eventually transformed as the sporting aspects were emphasized and the historical combative nature was downplayed.

The formation of the International Judo Federation in 1951 and the introduction of judo into the modern Olympic Games in 1964 were big steps in its growth. The first International Judo Championships took place in 1956 in Tokyo, Japan, with 31 athletes participating from 21 countries. By the 2003 World Championships in Osaka, Japan, there were 686 competitors from 102 countries.

The internationalization of competition dramatically influenced the course of judo development. Modern research and sports training principles were incorporated into judo training. Different countries adopted different training approaches with varying degrees of success. Judo techniques and tactics changed as the rules evolved. As more people practiced judo and the level of competition increased, the techniques and training were refined, with contest effectiveness as the ultimate measure of success.

According to the International Judo Federation (IJF), the world governing body for international judo competition, judo is undoubtedly the most popular combat sport and martial art in the world. There are 202 National Olympic Committees globally, and 187 Affiliated National Judo Federations, making it one of the most widespread of Olympic sports. More than 45 different countries have earned Olympic medals in judo, and 31 boast champions who have won gold medals in either the Olympics or World Championships.

Below: While judo is clearly rooted in traditional arts of war studied by the samurai, it is practiced today as a fun sport by millions of adults and children around the world.

JUDO SELF-DEFENSE TECHNIQUES

Jigoro Kano applied modern sport methodology to traditional *jujutsu* and found that it produced a better combat art because it added realism to the training by permitting full resistance from your opponent. Just as non-contact self-defense training will not provide the benefits of full-contact judo, training solely for sports contests will not provide complete self-defense training. The rules of judo competition provide a safe and challenging learning environment, but they also limit certain techniques that can be used in a real fight. This is why judo includes a number of non-competitive components.

Jigoro Kano was eager to preserve traditional self-defense techniques that could not be used safely in competition, including punches, kicks, knee locks, and other joint locks. These techniques, as well as modern ones like handgun defenses, are learned in *kata* practice.

Many people train in judo primarily for self-defense. In one online poll of more than 2700 people, 24 per cent said their main interest in judo was competition, while another 23 per cent said self-defense. Recreation or fun was the main interest of 19 per cent of the respondents, followed by physical fitness, character development, and other interests.

For those who have never used sport-training methods, or those who have never explored traditional *bujutsu* (martial arts) training, it is easy to discount the effectiveness of the other. But in judo we should continually seek opportunities to challenge ourselves by examining the weaknesses in our training and keeping our minds open to other methods. Competing against an opponent in a contest can be an effective method of training for self-defense, while practicing the *kata* helps to learn specific techniques adapted to self-defense situations in a controlled manner.

Despite its high profile as a sport, many people consider judo to be strictly a martial art, with a greater emphasis on self-defense or *kata* practice. There is a broad resurgence in the practice of *kata* around the world. It provides an alternative way to progress in the study of judo so that there is something for every age and interest. Over time, your interest in judo may change, often from competition in your youth to *kata* practice as you age.

JUDO TODAY

The steady progress towards judo as a sport that was made under Jigoro Kano has continued in the years since the creation of the International Judo Federation. Many people now think of judo simply as a sport because it is included along with other major sports in Olympic competition. Although many judo students around the world regularly practice various strikes, joint locks, and weapon defenses that are not permitted in competition, the emphasis on sport judo for the last 60 to 70 years has downplayed the significance of the full range of judo self-defense techniques preserved in the *kata*. As a result, the value of judo as a form of self-defense is sometimes misunderstood and underestimated.

Although still heavily influenced by the ideals of its founder, sport judo around the world today is quite different from what it was during its origins in 19th-century Japan. With the ever-growing popularization of sports in society and the downplaying of non-competition judo techniques, the question for judo in the 21st century is, "Are we fighting or playing?"

Other martial artists occasionally use the term sport to refer to judo as a game with no usefulness, implying it is only for play and cannot be effective for self-defense, fighting, or combat. Some martial artists even think the distinction between sport and martial art is that martial artists train for real life while sport judo athletes are bound by unrealistic rules designed to ensure safety rather than fighting effectiveness.

In fact, the distinction is more complex and rather surprising. One of the primary differences between the fighting effectiveness of a modern combat sport like judo and traditional martial arts like *jujutsu* is in the value of the training methods. Because of their potential danger or lethality, many martial arts techniques must be practiced with artificial—even counter-productive—methods. Slow, careful, non-contact training is not the most effective approach to prepare for actual fighting situations that usually require the opposite reactions.

The more potentially damaging a technique is, the more carefully and unrealistically it needs to be applied. For example, realistic training in throat strikes or eye gouges is seldom seen in martial arts classes, but is often recommended for self-defense.

Teaching these techniques may help judo students to understand intellectually what to do, but does not provide effective results for quick, reflexive, and accurate application against an unwilling opponent in real-life combat. They are simply too dangerous to practice repeatedly against a classmate.

By removing some of the potential dangers, sport training methods ironically lead to better results for the same type of combat skills. Sport more typically produces efficient, fast, and spontaneous reactions with full power. Sport training achieves results against a resistant opponent, who is also utilizing full power while engaging in strategic and tactical resistance, using all of his physical ability and training. Techniques that do not work are soon abandoned, and successful skills are honed against different attackers under a variety of conditions.

Maintaining control in various combat situations—both attack and defense—is difficult when faced with the unpredictable nature of an opponent's efforts. Facing these situations in contest or practice sparring (*randori*) prepares judo students for similar situations. Each opponent in competition is operating at the limit of physical and psychological skill. By pushing that limit, contestants are continually realizing and expanding their potential, preparing them mentally and physically for any serious conflict.

Training in martial arts is most effective when you can achieve objective results. It can be misleading to substitute your own subjective perception of effectiveness with a co-operating partner for an objective defeat of a resisting opponent. Practitioners of the older styles of *jujutsu* had a limited ability to train effectively for self-defense and combat during times of peace because they could not prepare for combat without severe risk to co-operative training partners. As a result, classical martial arts adopted highly stylized, ritualistic—even dysfunctional—training methods. Instead, modern combat sports like judo now provide the superior training in effective fighting techniques under real conditions.

Using sport competition as preparation for real fighting can be quite different from playing it as a game. Judo matches, along with *randori* in class, are simply different methods for training the mind and body to deal with fighting situations. This helps prepare students for anything they have to fight for—whether it is fighting for their country in the Olympics, their life on the street, or any worthy goal outside of judo.

Of course, sports training can go wrong. As Jigoro Kano warned, winning and losing can become too important and start to pervert the training process. The ultimate goal is not winning medals, which are just objective recognition of your progress and skill. Winning at all costs is less respected than good sportsmanship and trying your best so you leave the competition area having learned some valuable lessons. Competition itself—win or lose—is a powerful motivator and training tool that helps to develop character.

WHAT IS JUDO?

Judo is a fusion of ancient combat art, modern sports training, and a philosophy of continuous improvement. It is a complex combat system that preserves martial traditions and techniques of Japan, but is also a popular sport that clearly prepares the athlete for any physical confrontation off the mat. It is a safe and fun recreational activity that emphasizes building character. It is an art that allows free expression and displays the beauty of co-ordinated movement. It is a method of training the body and mind using principles that can also apply to how you lead your life. Both sport and martial art, judo has unique depth and strength not readily found in other sports or martial arts.

The give and take required in judo helps participants to develop good sportsmanship.

Progressing in judo

Judo is difficult to learn. Fortunately, it can also be fun. Judo is designed to be an activity anyone can participate in: from schoolchildren to seniors, from the most fit athletes to those who need to get in shape, able-bodied or physically challenged, male or female, big or small.

All students go through well-defined steps to learn the basics, and there are clear methods for working towards mastery. Whatever your limitations, success in judo can be achieved. Some of that success will only come through hard work, but much of it will come while enjoying the games, drills, free practice, and tournaments common to judo around the world. Judo students feel the exhilaration of succeeding through personal effort, the joy of achieving goals, and camaraderie with others facing the same battles.

Overcoming challenges is part of what makes judo so rewarding. Sprains, scrapes, sore muscles, and bruised egos are common in classes where beginners are learning methods of attack and defense. Some people experience emotions brought on by fatigue, defeat, or apparent lack of progress. Yet students also learn that obstacles of all types can be overcome, physical limitations can be extended, and fears can be faced. This is invaluable training for anyone striving to be confident and successful.

Learning judo is a growth process. As a beginner, you learn safety rules and falling skills. You progress to learning basic positions for throwing or pinning. When you feel confident in performing basic techniques, your training partner adds movement or resistance to make it more realistic, and you learn ways of defending against attacks. You then begin to make your moves more powerful and adaptable, and learn ways of combining techniques. Next you try to apply what you have learned in *randori*, in which your training partner tries to unbalance and weaken you. As you continue to learn more techniques and develop a greater depth of understanding of the techniques, you may be ready to test yourself in a tournament.

After each tournament or match you must re-examine your training, then redouble your efforts to study judo so you can perform better next time against an even more skilled opponent. Since every judo student is striving to improve, each brings other students along on the path to higher quality judo. You will continue to

Through concentrated effort, learn effortless action.

advance, perhaps exceeding your own expectations, because other students who are equally committed will help to push you to be the best that you can be.

Rely on your *sensei*, or experienced instructor, to help and guide you as you advance. The *sensei* usually has a better perspective on your training than you do, and can observe and judge your progress, awarding ranks to recognize achievements.

Judo is an endless path of self-discovery. It represents a journey with a definite beginning and middle, but no real end. The beginning is when you take your first few lessons, but the middle portion of the journey never ceases. A student who stays on the path will always be learning and advancing. Many judo masters continue to learn new things, and approach practice with the same awe and wonder they had as new students.

In judo you first learn to control your body, your emotions, and your mind; only then can you control your opponent. It is exciting the first time you throw a resisting opponent spontaneously and without effort, or hold or control someone so that he or she cannot escape from you or hurt you. As you improve you will see that throws that seem difficult can actually be done effortlessly, even against opponents bigger than you. The more you understand about judo and the more you improve your skill level, the more fun judo is. Imagine how wonderful it feels when judo techniques come easily and they work on even the toughest opponents. This level of skill requires years of practice and is usually recognized by the black belt.

What does a black belt really mean?

One of the questions most often asked by beginners is, "How long does it take to get a black belt in judo?" Most people want to hear that it takes just a year or two of attendance in class, but the truth is that misconceptions about what a black belt is tend to give students unrealistic expectations.

Today we see black belts worn by very young children, martial arts schools issuing contracts guaranteeing a black belt within a short time, mail-order black belts for sale in martial arts magazines, celebrities with honorary black belts, and demonstrations of black-belt skill involving walking on nails, swallowing swords, and other amazing feats. This raises general questions about the meaning of the black belt, and threatens the legitimacy of martial arts ranks.

The significance of the black belt rank may have been diluted over time in many martial arts systems, particularly due to commercialism, but the worldwide standard in judo has remained quite high. Jigoro Kano created the basic ranking system and recognition of ranks with colored belts still used in almost all martial arts today. This rank system replaced the traditional scrolls or diplomas used in older martial arts. The black belt was the first rank he created to signify completion of the first step of training, and there are ten levels of black belt for further advancement. Essentially, the black belt rank is a symbol of a student's graduation to another step in training—one that is even longer than the first step.

The first level of black belt is called *shodan*, which means "first level" or "beginning step." Promotion to black belt recognizes hard work and a level of accomplishment of which you can be proud. But *shodan* is just the beginning, or base, for learning the most important lessons of judo. It shows you are proficient at most of the techniques, but does not mean you have mastered judo.

To get a black belt you simply find a good teacher and begin training. A school in a convenient location helps you attend regularly, and a wide range of serious training partners also helps. Most importantly, you must devote yourself to practice and work hard. It is not easy, but it is a step-by-step training process, and you may attain the belt some day when you are no longer even looking for it. It could take a few years, or you may never achieve it. Black belt candidates realize that the belt is not as important as the lessons learned along the way.

Ranks are earned by the student, but awarded by the instructor. The instructor can recognize all the factors that make up a black belt and should be trusted to promote you when you have demonstrated the requirements. More than just the physical skills and techniques, these include conduct, character, maturity, and internalization of the principles of judo.

Applying judo principles to life outside judo school is something that brings black belts together. This is one of the reasons Jigoro Kano renamed his style of *jujutsu* judo.

Adversity does not cause a judo student to wither, it helps the student flourish.

Do means the way, path or road that students of judo follow. In other words, it is more than just the activity that takes place on the mat. As a judo black belt, you will understand how the principles that you have learned in class can improve your character and the rest of your life. For example, when you learn through experience to be committed to a judo throw and to follow through to completion, you become conscious of how these same fundamentals can help you to achieve other goals off the mats.

Continuously striving for perfection as a whole person is a sign of the black belt. This is not to say that black belts do not have faults—they are just the ones working on improving themselves. All judo black belts would affirm how learning judo has helped them change their lives for the better. The belt simply represents their personal struggle to achieve excellence.

Students who are overly concerned with getting promotions often discourage easily when they realize it is harder than they expected. Those who strive for excellence without concern for rank often do well; they are not affected by temporary setbacks or discouraged by unrealistic expectations. The road to black belt begins with enthusiasm—if you have the persistence and dedication to pursue ever-greater accomplishments your enthusiasm will only grow.

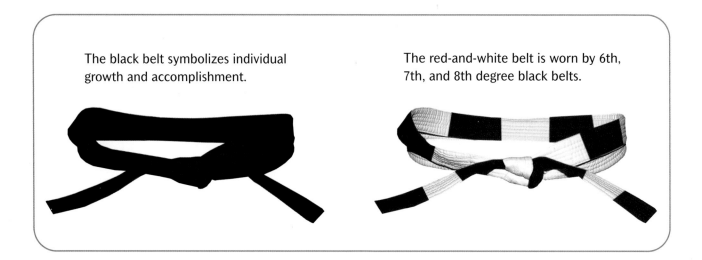

The black belt symbolizes individual growth and accomplishment.

The red-and-white belt is worn by 6th, 7th, and 8th degree black belts.

Goals of judo training

People have different goals for their participation in judo. These range from being the best in the world and winning a gold medal at the Olympics to learning basic self-defense, just having fun, or developing self-confidence so you will not be afraid. As you advance in judo your goals may change. One of the wonderful things about judo is that there are multiple levels of principles and goals: a beginner can focus on mastering a single hip throw, while a more advanced student doing the same hip throw gains insight into the larger meaning of judo.

Judo in a narrow sense is the study of the most efficient and effective methods of attack and defense. One goal of judo as physical education is to develop a healthy mind and body that work harmoniously together. Another is to work with others in synergy so everyone benefits. Ultimately, by striving for perfection you can contribute something of value and improve the world we live in. Essentially, the goals of judo involve improving yourself physically, mentally, and morally. They also involve ethical and social principles that Jigoro Kano believed were implicit by-products of judo training.

Below: Judo teaches you to be present on the battlefield of life, ready to meet any challenge.

How to learn judo

Judo is designed so that anyone can be proficient. The training methods and physical principles that make judo work apply to women and men equally, and to all ages from young children to senior citizens. They work for people with a variety of challenges— a strong component of the Paralympic Games is the judo competition for blind athletes. No one is too tall or too short, too heavy or too light, too strong or too weak. People of all backgrounds from all parts of the world practice judo with minimal equipment. The most basic requirement is the will to learn.

In the beginning

The way to learn judo is through training—that is, to become proficient with specialized instruction and practice. You cannot achieve this on your own. To become skilled in judo you must find an instructor to teach you and other students with whom to practice. The online resources listed on page 156 can help you with that. The choice of a school, or *dojo*, may vary depending on your age, interests, and condition, but since there are many experienced judo teachers, or *sensei*, it should not be hard to locate one near you.

In addition to a *dojo* with proper mats, you need a *judogi*, or practice uniform. Your *sensei* will usually be able to recommend one and help you get it. The *judogi* is loose and comfortable to exercise in, but made of very strong cotton fabric. It is an essential tool used to control and throw an opponent. The traditional *judogi* is white, but competitors may also need a blue *judogi*.

Enter the *dojo* with a positive attitude, ready to try your best. From the first class you will begin to learn some of the safety rules and etiquette of judo. Classes customarily begin with a bow intended to show your respect and thanks to your *sensei* and training partners, who are helping you learn. This is followed by a warm-up period before training begins with falling, or *ukemi*.

Ukemi is the art of breaking your fall to land safely when thrown to the mat. It is an important skill to master in order to provide a stimulating involvement in judo. *Ukemi* is also valuable to protect yourself off the mat.

Being able to fall comfortably and with confidence frees the mind and relaxes the body so you can attempt more difficult moves. It is difficult to enjoy judo practice if you are afraid of falling, or you get hurt while falling. As most people are afraid of falling, it takes considerable practice and specific skills to overcome this obstacle.

There are many types of *ukemi*, but essentially you need to develop the ability to fall in any direction and land safely. Judo throwing techniques should only be practiced with a person who is skillful in *ukemi*.

Judo practice alone will improve your fitness level, but the better condition you are in, the better you will be at judo. Most serious athletes supplement their sports training with weight training, running, or other vigorous exercise; judo athletes are no exception.

Safety must always be a consideration in practice if judo is to bring you long-term health benefits, not injuries. Because judo is a very effective combat sport, some of the techniques can hurt a classmate if they are not applied carefully and properly. Dangerous techniques should not be practiced outside class or on someone who is unprepared. In class, safety requires everyone to focus on what he or she is doing, and to treat training partners with care. Your approach to practice should always be conscientious and determined.

Types of judo training

The primary types of traditional judo training are *kata* and *randori*. *Shiai*, or contest, is a special form of *randori*. In addition, there are many forms of drills, games, and exercises to develop specific skills, which can be applied in one of the other forms of practice.

KATA

Kata means "form," and is a method of practicing with a co-operating partner in a prearranged fashion, following a basic pattern created by experts to teach specific skills and combative principles. It is often seen as a formal demonstration, in special *kata* tournaments, or as an advanced rank promotion requirement, but is also an important exercise in judo class. It is in the practice of *kata* that you develop a wide range of judo skills—including different throws, joint locks, combat ranges, striking, and pressure points—seldom used or not allowed in *randori* or *shiai*. Students learn to apply techniques to both sides in response to a diverse set of attacks, which even include an assortment of weapons such as guns or knives.

The groupings of the types of *kata* recognized by the Kodokan Judo Institute in Tokyo (*see* box, right) may help judo students to understand the basic role of each *kata*, but this does not imply that the *kata* strictly adheres to the title of the grouping. All of the *kata* are designed for physical education, careful study of attack and defence, and understanding the theories of judo.

The *randori no kata* are the most commonly practiced *kata* because they involve the techniques that are most often performed in free practice and they complement the study of many

popular throwing and grappling techniques. The techniques included in the *randori no kata* are listed on page 152. The other *kata* are usually learned after achieving the black belt rank.

The Kodokan *kata* help preserve a worldwide standard for judo techniques and theory. Practicing them provides students with a connection to Jigoro Kano and others who devised them. They help with in-depth study of techniques with a partner learning the same techniques, so that you develop co-operative skills to balance the competitive ones learned in other forms of training. Co-operation in *kata* practice does not mean your training partner is acting a part; it just means that *uke* (person receiving the technique) has agreed to perform certain attacks in a specified manner. Each attack *uke* makes is intended to be successful and it is up to *tori* (person performing the technique) to apply the proper defense.

A comprehensive study of *kata* also consists of important combat concepts such as the concentration of spirit (*kiai*), judgment of engagement distance (*maai*), performance of appropriate action in conformance with combat theory (*riai*), and the establishment of a special kind of alertness to dominate the opponent (*zanshin*). If all the techniques comprise the alphabet of judo, then *kata* represents the complete words, as well as the basic grammar and sentence structure.

RANDORI

Students practicing *randori*, or free practice, are learning to use the letters, words, and sentences of judo to communicate in a meaningful way. The meaning of the Japanese word *randori* suggests there is generally no controlling form or pre-established method of practice. It is often practiced freely, with each person attacking and defending at will with full power. At other times it is practiced lightly with less resistance, or with other restrictions to train in a particular area of study (for example, only one person attacking while the other practises defense). The level of resistance and effort in *randori* should always be adjusted to the size and ability of your partner, so that you work harder against larger or more skilled partners and stay lighter against smaller or less skilled partners.

Practice partners in *randori* are often competing to gain the advantage and do not know what the other will do, so they must be prepared to make quick judgments and act decisively. Jigoro Kano wrote about the "hundreds of valuable lessons" of *randori* in *Kodokan Judo*:

In randori one can never be sure what technique the opponent will employ next, so he must be constantly on guard. Being alert becomes second nature. One acquires poise, the self-confidence that comes from knowing that he can cope with any eventuality. The powers of attention and observation, imagination, of reasoning and judgment are naturally heightened, and these are all useful attributes in daily life as well as in the dojo.

It is generally accepted by judo experts, including Jigoro Kano, that *randori* must be given priority in your training. It adds an element of realism to judo and should be the mainstay of practice time once you have learned the basics. *Randori* involves a complex mental and physical relationship between the participants that *kata* cannot achieve. There is a huge difference between learning how to do a technique with a co-operating partner and being able to apply it with minimum effort against a well-trained, resisting opponent. Only in *randori* do you learn how to take advantage of opportunities created by your opponent's movements, reactions, posture, strength, and composure. *Randori* is more about constantly improving yourself than doing everything right, so do not be afraid to try a variety of techniques.

Randori is driven by the energy of discovery born of risk and error. As you attempt to attack you will often fail, but as Jigoro Kano said, "When you fall down seven times, get up eight." *Randori* is the time to create opportunities and see possibilities, overcoming your limitations. The value of judo is gained, like food, only upon digestion and assimilation. It can only be appreciated through experience—and *randori* provides the practical, free environment to experience all that judo has to offer. Eventually, *randori* will lead to a new understanding of proper technique, and a state of awareness that allows quick, reflexive, and decisive action. Rather than thinking about your next move, it is better to be so present in the realities of the moment so you simply act in harmony with the flow of the match.

Sharpen your sword in *randori* so that it will be capable of one swift cut when needed.

Top tips for *randori*

Success in *randori* is one sign that a student is ready for the black belt rank. Here is some of the most common advice judo teachers give to help students with their *randori*.

- There is no score or winner in *randori*, so banish thoughts of victory or defeat.
- Focus on attacking freely without regard for being thrown.
- Keep a relaxed and natural posture to retain free movement of your body and mind.
- Keep your arms loose.
- Keep your head up and centered over your hips.
- Do not waste energy.
- Follow through with each technique; do not get in the habit of going half way.
- Follow up each technique with another.
- Never refuse a practice partner.
- Seek out training partners who are better than you.
- Try new moves to overcome problem situations.
- Use *kiai* (concentration of your spirit in a shout) for extra power.
- Rely on skill and timing, not strength.
- Control your breathing.
- Keep your elbows close to your body where they are most powerful and least vulnerable.
- Always face your opponent.
- Do not cross your feet when moving around.
- Get the strongest grip you can, and never fail to get a grip.
- Learn to feel your partner's intentions and anticipate attacks.
- Maintain *mizu no kokoro* (mind like water); stay calm and undisturbed.
- Focus on *kuzushi* (breaking balance) to create opportunities for attacks.
- Employ the principle of maximum efficiency even when you could easily overpower the opponent with size or strength.
- Help your partner to learn while you perfect your technique.
- Act now; analyze later.
- Do not make excuses; do not give up. Tomorrow you will be better.

SHIAI

Shiai, or contest, is the form of judo practice you should spend the least amount of time doing. Nonetheless, it is also a vital component of a well-developed course in judo. In tournaments you use all your previous preparation and training to try to overcome an opponent who is also doing his or her best to challenge you. Even in small local tournaments the pressure to succeed creates a very different environment from friendly *randori*.

Valuable lessons can be learned in *shiai*, including some that cannot be gained in other forms of practice. Judo is a unique face-to-face form of individual competition involving full-contact attack and defense. Fighting is an acquired skill, but learning to stand up to others and to fight fairly and with resolve for what you believe in will serve you well not only in judo but throughout life.

One purpose of competition in judo is to take the place of the older *shinken shobu* (life-and-death fights) in developing your technique, knowledge, and character. You never see yourself so clearly as when you face your own death. Judo competition can provide a safe, controlled glimpse of this kind of defeat—and the level of effort required to win.

Fighting spirit can really only be developed through fighting. Certainly, judo competition is not the same as the battlefield, but it serves a similar purpose, and it is closer to a combat situation than any other safe form of training for the ordinary person.

Judo students should be aware that winning at all costs is not the proper attitude for entering judo *shiai*. When used as a training method, judo competition is not about winning or losing; it is about giving your best effort and improving yourself, challenging yourself to stretch beyond your own self-imposed limits. No one ever developed any real confidence without first overcoming significant personal challenges.

Participating in *shiai* is like placing a red-hot blade under the hammer of a swordsmith to sharpen it. In this sense it is a form of *seishin tanren*, or spiritual forging. It is about testing yourself and helping your opponent to do the same. By testing your skills under pressure you learn to improve your level of ability, focus your preparation and training, and strengthen your mental toughness. This further increases the self-confidence and fighting spirit being developed during *kata* and *randori* practice.

The rules of judo competition have changed considerably since the first Kodokan Red and White Tournament was held in 1884. At first, Kodokan judo was seen as a form of *jujutsu* and matches were held in the older *jujutsu* style. An early participant in these matches, Sakujiro Yokoyama, is quoted as saying:

In those days contests were extremely rough and frequently cost the participants their lives. Thus, whenever I sallied forth to take part in any of those affairs, I invariably bade farewell to my parents, since I had no assurance that I should ever return alive.

The rules of judo were created by Jigoro Kano, but have been revised many times. Locks of the fingers, toes, wrists, and ankles were banned in contests in 1899. In 1916, *ashi garami* (knee entanglement, twisting knee lock) and *dojime* (trunk/kidney squeeze with the legs) were also banned in competition. Joint lock attacks in judo contests were limited to the elbow in 1925. Over the years other rules have also been created to ensure the safety of contestants—such as the banning of *kani basami* (flying scissors) after this lock broke Japanese champion Yasuhiro Yamashita's ankle.

Judo matches originally had no weight categories and no time limit. It was not until 1964 that judo competition was divided into three weight classes. The World Championship finals still lasted up to 15 minutes until the 1970s. As judo became more and more popular, the number of weight classes increased to eight for the World

As you progress in judo, continue to challenge yourself by seeking better competition.

Championships, and match times were reduced to the current five-minute limit. Only the All Japan Championships are still conducted with no weight classes.

Since 1964, judo competition has been recognized as an event in the Olympic Games, which takes place every four years. Every two years (in odd-numbered years) the International Judo Federation (IJF) hosts the Judo World Championships.

The IJF is recognized by the International Olympic Committee as the international governing body for Olympic judo. Since 1952 it has established the rules of judo competition, promoted judo around the world, sanctioned international tournaments, trained referees, and administered the sport. Each country has a national judo organization that is a member of the IJF. As a result, the rules of judo *shiai* are very consistent around the world, except for special safety rules for children or novices that may vary from country to country. A guide to the IJF rules is included on pages 152–153.

Other forms of training

Beginners usually start learning judo techniques with partners in a form of practice that is called *uchikomi*, or repetition training, performed in a co-operative fashion to achieve the basic movement patterns. This is the first step to gaining the physical co-ordination and understanding of a throw or other judo technique. It consists of entering into the position for applying a technique, usually a throw, but stopping short of executing it. Repeating the movement over and over again gets the throw ingrained into the muscles and mind so that the essential preparatory movements of the throw can be done quickly and spontaneously, without thinking.

Uchikomi allows you to learn new throws when you do not yet have sufficient control to complete them safely. Even after you are skilled in a throw, *uchikomi* is a popular form of practice because you get many repetitions focusing on some important elements of a technique—such as breaking balance or the application of power—without much falling for your training partner.

While *uchikomi* is repetition of the movements entering into a technique, *nagekomi* is the repeated practice of the entire throwing technique. In *nagekomi*, you repeatedly throw your opponent to the mat so the practice includes the vital application and follow through for each technique. A landing mat, or crash pad, may be used to make the falls more comfortable and to protect both partners.

Yakusoku geiko is an agreed-upon or controlled form of practice where participants decide in advance what the conditions will be. One traditional method of apply-

ing this to *randori* is to agree to practice throws without resistance from the partner while alternating attackers, so that each person gets a turn to practice a variety of throws. Practice partners may also agree to allow a certain degree of resistance, or allow throw avoidance but not counter throws, or any other restriction to focus the training on the desired area of practice.

Many forms of drills have been devised to train participants in particular skills of judo, such as gripping, turning over an opponent on the ground, throwing while moving, and so on. Especially since modern sports methodology has been used to train Olympic judo athletes, advances in sports sciences—including physiology and psychology—have added new concepts to some of the traditional judo training methods for high-level competitors. Anyone training for competition can benefit from these advances in scientific sports training methods.

As an example, the principle of specificity requires that training conditions be as close as possible to actual competition in order to maximize the effect of the training. For the training to produce the desired results, drills should allow skills to be repeated safely and in their entirety, while being realistic and reflecting the conditions under which the acquired skills will be used.

Various forms of *randori* or *nagekomi* have been devised to train repetitively in a specific aspect of judo competition. For example, one person can be designated the attacker while the other practices defence, or a student can work for a designated period of time against a particular defence (like stiff-arming) to attempt numerous skills for defeating it. A good judo coach has ways of training athletes for each distinct skill or competitive tactic that needs to be strengthened. For maximum transference to real competition, these drills should duplicate the specific biomechanics, neuromuscular patterns, pressures, and other conditions commonly faced in competition.

Judo training helps you to be self-disciplined, attentive, and considerate of others; the more you practice these character traits outside class, the better.

Tips for solo practice

Judo students often wonder how they can practice without a partner. A general strength and conditioning programme is beneficial, and all serious judo students should try to improve their fitness levels with additional training outside class. Although most judo techniques require a practice partner, there are a few ways to improve some skills by yourself.

- Practice the footwork needed to enter for throws. Try placing bricks in front of you to represent your opponent's feet, then repeatedly step or jump into position for various hip, leg, or shoulder throws. Try the same steps with your hands against a wall, or in a swimming pool with your legs under water.
- Tie a bicycle tire inner tube (or your judo belt) around a post or tree. Grab one end with each hand, and practice entering for your favorite throw as in *uchikomi*. A thousand repetitions will improve the strength, speed, and accuracy of your entry. This can be done with cable weights to improve strength, or with the inner tube tied to something that moves (like an open door handle) to improve balance.
- To practice judo techniques, many students buy grappling dummies—commercially produced mannequins with lifelike weight, movable joints, and a tough exterior. They are especially useful for repetitive drills on the ground.

Remember, perfect technique comes only from perfect practice. When a teacher is not around, do not develop bad habits. Constantly examine your practice to ensure you are performing each move correctly.

Left: Grab the belt as if it is your opponent's jacket and practice entering for throws with good posture and driving power.

Below: Using bricks in various positions as though they were your opponent's feet, jump into different throws to increase speed, accuracy, and balance.

Why judo works

Judo instruction stresses application over theory. A real understanding of the principles that make judo work is revealed slowly through long and arduous practice. Full comprehension does not come from intellectual investigation as much as from physical application, which can only be achieved through proper training. However, you can proceed with the knowledge that there is a sound basis for each technique. At the heart of judo strategy is the premise that sheer size and raw strength are no match for balance, skill, and flexibility.

Scientific basis

Judo is a modern combat sport based on scientific principles. A principle is simply a rule explaining the functioning of a natural phenomenon.

Jigoro Kano explained the effectiveness of seemingly impossible feats with simple explanations based on sound physics and psychology. Judo teachers today still stress proper technique over excessive force to achieve an objective. Good technique means the sound application of strength and other resources in accordance with natural laws and principles that maximize the results of your efforts. It is this emphasis on technique that allows a smaller person with proper training to defeat a larger or stronger person.

Many scientific principles apply to judo. Consider, for instance, Newton's laws of motion written in 1686, exactly 20 years after he developed the theory of gravity (which is also quite important in judo). Newton's laws of motion are critical to understanding how to keep your balance, or how to unbalance an opponent in preparation for a throw.

Newton's first law of motion states that every object will remain at rest, or in uniform motion in a straight line, unless compelled to change its state by the action of an external force. This is normally taken as the definition of inertia, which is a major obstacle to overcome when you are trying to throw someone from a static position. Applied to judo, it means that a moving opponent will tend to continue moving, so when you are executing a forward throw it is most efficient simply to stop your opponent's feet from advancing while his or her upper body continues effortlessly in the direction it was moving. This unbalances your opponent, regardless of size, without the use of strength.

Newton's second law of motion explains that an object will only accelerate or decelerate if a force is acting on it. The law defines the force to be equal to the change in momentum (mass times velocity) over time. In other words, if your own body mass is moving sharply towards your opponent, the amount of force exerted on your opponent will be determined by your size, speed, and how quickly you decelerate into your opponent. Remember that your own momentum being applied as a force to your opponent is often an important factor in causing your opponent to lose balance—which is your objective. Using your own momentum is more efficient than simply using isolated muscles to create the same amount of force.

Although these laws of nature are much more involved, they are learned almost intuitively in judo through physical experimentation and instruction. Additional study and careful scientific analysis can improve your performance and heighten your appreciation of the complexities inherent in physical combat.

Physical concepts utilized in judo include gravity, leverage, inertia, force, friction, velocity, acceleration, power, stability, and momentum. If you understand how your anatomical center of gravity, muscular rigidity, and other factors affect balance, it may be easier to learn to apply throws and other skills. Similarly, a study of basic anatomy, biomechanics, and kinesiology is useful for understanding how joint locks are applied, how to make strangulations work, or where to apply pressure on the body to achieve the maximum result.

Even for beginners concentrating on becoming skillful at falling, fundamental scientific rules, such as the dissipation of energy, can explain why certain falling methods are used. Judo teachers need a solid understanding of these principles to communicate the reasons for each movement, to validate training exercises, or to show how judo works.

Psychological principles are also at work in judo. They can help provide an understanding of your opponent's response times under various conditions, the predictability of your opponent's reactions to your attacks or other stimuli, the effect of your mental state on performance, concentration techniques, ways to mentally unbalance your opponent, and so on.

For example, if you are successful in instilling fear, uncertainty, or doubt in your opponent, this will certainly improve your ability to attack freely. Likewise, you will need to maintain a strong sense of confidence if you are to prevent your opponent from creating doubts in your own mind. After learning some of the physical techniques, an awareness of the mental aspects of judo becomes important if you are to progress and succeed in competition.

Judo is as much a science as it is an art. There is room for individual stylistic expression, and to appreciate the gracefulness and beauty of judo, but the core of judo is its effectiveness: a judo technique must work in the real world. Acting in accordance with the physical laws of the universe is essential if you are to achieve the maximum result from your efforts.

Use science to improve your judo

Here are some specific principles judo students use to maximize their effectiveness.

- Focus the power of your entire body onto one part of your opponent's body to gain an advantage.
- When faced with unstoppable power, yield and give way in order to use your opponent's power against him or her.
- Apply your energy in the direction your opponent is moving.
- Exploit leverage to maximize your strength.
- Attack your opponent's weakness with your strength to gain victory.
- Keep your opponent moving to build momentum.
- Maintain flexibility in your body to help keep your balance.
- Pull when pushed, push when pulled.
- Move quickly to gain a position of relative advantage.
- Get under your opponent's center of gravity to attack.
- Keep your own center of gravity low to defend.
- Keep a wide base when on the ground.
- Keep your body loose so the effect of your opponent's force can be localized and nullified.
- Utilize your full body length as one unit to gain the greatest leverage.
- Use your full body mass, not just the strength of your arms or legs, to increase power.
- Concentrate all of your power at the moment of attack.
- Increase the force available for attacks through speed.
- Overwhelming strength can only be used against you if you try to oppose it.

Maximum effect with minimum effort (*seiryoku zen'yo*)

After examining the principles affecting performance in judo, Jigoro Kano formulated one overriding principle that defines good technique. This innovation separated judo from all previous martial arts, and has been adopted by most sports training programs today. Often called the maximum efficiency principle, or *seiryoku zen'yo*, it states that the goal of judo technique is to obtain the greatest possible result for the amount of energy invested.

Achieving maximum effect with minimum effort requires just the right amount of force to be exerted to accomplish the desired result. Too little is not ideal, nor is too much. One common misunderstanding of this principle is that the use of strength or force is always negative. Certainly, misapplication, unnecessary use, or excessive use of strength in a way that wastes energy is not desirable. But considerable strength may be essential, even when applied correctly, against a large or strong opponent of equal skill. Technique will overcome strength or size, but the larger the imbalance in size or strength, the greater your skill level will have to be relative to your opponent.

The physical education aspects of judo ensure the development of a strong, well co-ordinated body, but most top athletes today supplement judo practice with strength training. This is because the development of power improves competitive performance and is a critical component of technique. Naturally, power must be applied correctly in accord with proper leverage and bio-mechanics. The goal is the maximum efficient use of power, or the best use of energy.

One key aspect of this principle is the concept of *kuzushi*, or breaking balance. The idea is that you can maximize the result of any attack on an opponent whose balance is broken, whereas an opponent who retains control of his or her balance can easily move or resist successfully. The careful study of *kuzushi* is perhaps the most important element of learning successful throwing and grappling skills.

Flexibility and adaptability are also key components of judo. Your arms should be strong like chains, but loose enough to bend at a moment's notice. Similarly, your legs should be powerful, but able to move with lightning speed. And finally, your mental state must be determined, yet relaxed enough to change direction. This is the essence of judo—the right application of strength, at the right time, and in the right place.

You progress not through what has been done, but by reaching toward what has yet to be done. It is by what you do today that you succeed tomorrow. Such is the virtue of practice.

Learn proper technique so that you can use your energy in the most efficient way.

How judo develops character

Judo is much more than just physical training; it is essentially a way to develop the mind and body so they can work harmoniously together. The emphasis in class is always on the physical aspects, but there are additional benefits in terms of developing a strong and healthy character. The struggle of judo training refines the self, but also benefits others. Offering yourself to your training partner requires complete trust and engenders mutual respect. Even top international competitors train together to become better. By honing their own skills, they help their rivals to improve.

The moral and ethical underpinnings of judo, inherited partly from Japanese warrior tradition, provide a way to consider judo as a larger activity than what takes place on the mat.

The principles of judo are multi-dimensional: they apply not only to physical skills, but to other parts of life too. When you maximize your efforts, you are practicing judo. Developing your character and striving to improve is a way of practicing judo. Working for the welfare of others and contributing to the betterment of the world is the ultimate way of practicing judo.

Mental approach to training

Judo cultivates, even requires, a positive can-do attitude. Practice will reinforce the understanding that results come from personal effort, and that great achievements can be made with enough determination. A step-by-step approach to mastering the physical skills gradually builds character traits that will make you successful in other areas of life as well. Since the purpose of judo is to subdue an opponent, it is vital to approach it with a serious attitude. Take your training seriously at all times for safety and maximum benefit.

The laws of nature must be fully experienced to be understood; they cannot be bent to the preconceived ideas of the observer. To master judo you must move in a natural manner, which means surrendering yourself to the way things are, rather than the way you would like them to be. This discovery of the natural principles of judo must be an intensely personal revelation achieved through intense training. Only when you apply yourself whole-heartedly to the training will you gain glimpses of meaning and higher principles. As Jigoro Kano wrote, "If there is effort, there is always accomplishment."

It is not uncommon for students to consider giving up practice because of lack of success in competition, unavailability of practice partners, a perceived lack of progress, injury, personal problems outside of class, or other concerns. These are simply additional obstacles to overcome in learning judo and developing self-discipline. Setting goals is often helpful, whether it is for proficiency in a particular technique, achieving a black belt rank, or defeating an opponent in competition. The successful student is one who climbs over, moves around, or knocks down each barrier. Of course, in conformance with the meaning of *ju* (flexibility), no set course of action will work against every obstacle.

> *It may well be said that the primary objective of practicing judo is perfection of character.*
>
> — H Seichiro Okazaki

Character lessons

There are lessons to be learned in studying most physical activities. When the lessons in judo are applied to everyday living, they help to elevate our life experience. Such lessons include discipline, perseverance, loyalty, the importance of flexibility, understanding the relationship between success and efforts expended, and working through the process of training to achieve excellence.

With no team to rely on or hold you back, judo is more of an individual achievement than many other sporting activities. It is hard to blame others or to get undeserved credit in judo. This leads to a sense of personal responsibility for your actions. It does not mean that others cannot push you to greater heights (or steer you in the wrong direction), but in judo your performance is a direct result of your own ability, preparation, and fighting spirit. You cannot use equipment to gain an advantage, and there is nothing to hide behind when you fail; it is a face-to-face form of combat that shapes character.

Beginners often think judo experts are tough—and they are right. However, to beginners this means that they can dish out punishment at will and never be defeated. In popular culture, the toughest martial artist is the one who can beat up all the others, but this represents a misconception about the toughness that judo engenders. The truth is quite the opposite. The toughness of a judo expert is a direct result of perseverance through harsh trials. It is better measured by the punishment you can take than by the punishment you can give. One value in judo training is the opportunity to test yourself and push yourself to your limits, continually expanding your limits and extending your capabilities.

Judo is a science implying mastery of various laws of nature, but it is also an art. The true value of any art form—whether judo, music, or sculpture—is its goal of discovering and developing the artist's true potential. Judo is a method of self-realization and expression. Its fundamental techniques, practice methods, philosophy, and moral basis are consistent with the free pursuit of insights into the self and the development of a strong individual character.

With even a little introspection, you will see the benefits of training in attack and defense. The qualities you will master include patience, perseverance, optimism, dependability, honesty, thoughtfulness, adaptability, independence, humility, courage, discipline, self-reliance, intensity, sincerity, flexibility, and co-operation. Other traits developed through judo are self-respect, deliberation, kindness, composure, and self-control. All of this can be summed up by one of the goals of judo practice: *jika no kansei*, or to strive for perfection as a whole person.

Recognize that the real battle is inside yourself.

Mutual welfare and benefit (*jita kyoei*)

Judo is about more than personal development. If your focus is always on yourself you will grow out of balance and become selfish. Jigoro Kano realized that achieving personal excellence depends to a great extent on others. For this reason he created the maxim *jita kyoei* to express his belief that the objective of self-development is to contribute something of value to the world. *Jita kyoei* is often translated as "mutual welfare and benefit," but more literally means "you and I shining together," or "mutual prosperity for self and others." All practice must be in conformance with this tenet of judo.

It goes without saying that the reckless study of attack and defense can result in injury. When you practice with a partner you are giving him your body and relying on him to take care of you. This requires a level of dependence and trust that cannot be achieved without genuine caring about your partner. Ideally, every form of judo practice has a benefit for both parties. Even while someone is practicing techniques on you, your attention should be focussed on learning the aspects of the attacks that are most effective for your own use, as well as the weaknesses that can be exploited to counter attack.

Learning to hold an opponent down and learning to escape from the hold are the opposite sides of the same technique. Learning how to fall for each throw is an essential step in learning how to perform the throws. Most people learn lessons by initially losing in tournaments, but gradually go on to win. Like a circle, you and your training partner are linked together into a whole, and we all depend on others to try their best so we can improve. This leads to a greater understanding of our interconnectedness and social responsibility.

In judo we seek the state of equilibrium that is called balance. In a dynamic world this harmony can never be achieved in isolation; you must learn how to work with other people. By studying the art of attack and defense you learn to resolve conflicts and contribute to peace.

Even as a newborn baby gasps its first precious breath, it learns it is on its own. Although it is totally dependent on others, the infant believes that it must fight for survival. In judo, too, we rely on others to show us the way, but each student must have the will to fight. Progress comes primarily as a result of individual effort, but is best achieved when we are challenged and assisted by others. Developing our strength, intellect, and morality ultimately has little value unless used in a positive way to benefit society. Just as a baby begins teaching others about life as soon as it is born, even though it struggles to learn the most basic things, we all have something to give, even as we all have something to learn from others.

Classification of techniques (waza)

Waza refers to the methods used to overcome greater strength and size with skill, timing, and agility. There are many ways to perform a particular technique depending on the strategic objective, the relative sizes and positions of the contestants, the strength or speed of the person applying the technique, and personal preferences.

It is important to learn a variety of techniques so you will be prepared to take advantage of any opportunity. Most competitors develop favorite techniques, or *tokui waza*, to a point that they can be applied with confidence against any type of opponent. But even favorite techniques often rely on strategies to trick or force the opponent into a vulnerable position for the attack. Other attacks, at least the threat of other attacks, are used to set up the opponent so your favourite throw will work. The larger your arsenal of techniques, the more opportunities you will be able to create.

There are three main types of *waza* (techniques):

- all throws used to get an opponent to the ground with force;
- grappling techniques—usually (not always) used on the ground;
- striking techniques used only for self-defense.

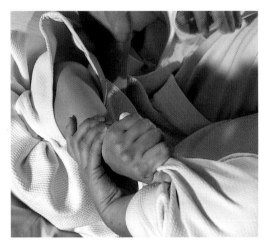
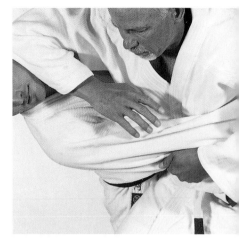

Practicing different types of techniques permits an appropriate level of response to control any threat.

Throwing (*nage waza*)

There are 67 basic throwing techniques defined by the Kodokan, and a nearly infinite number of variations. The *gokyo no waza* is the standard syllabus of judo throws originated by the founder of judo in 1895 at the Kodokan. From 1920 to 1982 the Kodokan *gokyo no waza* comprised 40 throws in five groups. On its 100th anniversary in 1982, an additional eight traditional judo throws that had been taken out in 1920 were reinstated and 17 new techniques were recognized as official Kodokan judo throws in a group called *shinmeisho no waza*. In 1997 the Kodokan added two more throws to the *shinmeisho no waza*. The 67 throwing techniques (*nage waza*) currently recognized by the Kodokan are shown on page 147.

Standard throwing techniques are divided into *waza* executed from a standing position (*tachi waza*) and sacrifice techniques executed while falling down (*sutemi waza*). There are three types of standing techniques, depending on the primary part of the body used to make the throw: hip throws (*koshi waza*), hand or arm throws (*te waza*) and foot or leg throws (*ashi waza*). Sacrifice throws are divided into those to the rear (*ma sutemi waza*) and those to the side (*yoko sutemi waza*).

These classifications describe the main element that makes a throw work in its classical form, but when techniques are performed differently from the traditional version, they may not appear consistent with the category in which they are classified. Many throws have been modified, or specialized variations created specifically for modern competition. For example, the shoulder wheel (*kata guruma*) is recognized as a hand throw, but is frequently performed in competition as a sacrifice throw, yet it retains its name because of the basic throwing action of wheeling your opponent over your shoulder.

Grappling (*katame waza*)

Grappling techniques are methods of controlling your opponents so they are forced to submit and co-operate because they are immobilized, threatened with injury, or rendered unconscious. Grappling techniques can be expected to end a match or confrontation conclusively. They involve the closest possible range of combat where other techniques are less effective.

When grappling techniques are performed on the ground they are called *ne waza*. Many can also be executed while standing, or used to force an opponent onto the ground. They are divided into pinning techniques (*osaekomi waza*), strangulations or choking techniques (*shime waza*), and joint locks (*kansetsu waza*). All can be used to force submission in different ways.

Osaekomi waza involves pinning your opponent to the ground so he or she cannot get away, whereas you are free to escape if desired. Most judo pins control your opponent so that he is helpless and vulnerable with his back on the ground, but in the judo *kata* there are also times when your opponent is held face down.

Shime waza includes chokes and strangles with the arms and the legs, as well as wrapping the *judogi* collar around the opponent's neck. Your opponent can be quickly rendered unconscious with a properly applied strangle. Often the more he resists, the more quickly the strangle works.

Although *kansetsu waza* includes any kind of joint lock (even neck or spine locks), only joint locks to the elbow are allowed in free practice or competition today because of the increased risk of injury when using locks to other joints. Other joint locks (such as knee and finger locks) are still practised in judo, usually by more advanced students, as part of various *kata*.

Striking (*atemi waza*)

Striking techniques are used to disable, distract, or unbalance your opponent in self-defense, but are not permitted in modern judo competition or *randori*. For safety they are usually practiced in *kata* form and are considered specialized techniques for study after attaining black belt. They are seldom practiced in judo classes or required for promotion, so are not demonstrated in this book.

Striking is a long-range fighting skill. Judo strategy calls for closing the distance and gaining control over your opponent. The closer your opponent is, the more difficult it is to make a powerful strike and the less important striking skills are. *Atemi waza* are often used to make the transition to a close-contact range of fighting so you can use throws, submissions, or control holds.

Strikes may be used to distract and break an opponent's balance, then combined with other techniques, such as throws. They are equally effective on the ground to weaken an opponent's defences and set up a more conclusive joint lock, submission or control hold.

Striking skills are divided into arm and hand strikes (*ude waza*) and foot or knee strikes (*ashi ate*). Sometimes the head may be used. Common strikes include punches, kicks, knee and elbow strikes, chops, and jabs.

Specific vital points are used as targets. Many are pressure points or sensitive areas that result in greater pain when struck. Some strikes can cause permanent damage. Certain strikes to the throat, eyes, bridge of the nose, kidneys, knees, and groin, for instance, can severely injure an opponent and are never practiced with full force contact.

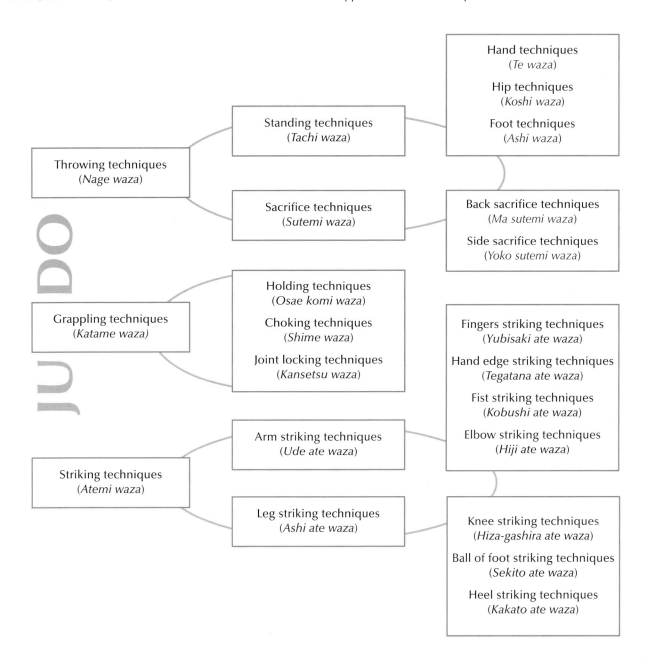

THROWING

Principles of throwing

Judo is not just a random collection of techniques. Progress comes from a real understanding, physically and mentally, of the principles involved in the various actions. A principle is a natural law or essential element of judo that is part of its intrinsic nature. Once learned, you can use the principle to solve problems you have not faced before.

You can learn a wide variety of meaningful principles by studying judo. Examples are the important elements of combat range or engagement distance (*maai*), proper technique (*waza*), and combat awareness (*zanshin*). These principles involve combat theories best learned from a standing position, although they apply equally when on the ground with an opponent.

All judo matches start standing. Keeping your own balance is a vital first step to protect yourself or get away from an attack. The next step, unbalancing your opponent, requires skill in gripping, posture, and movement control, but once learned, the art of throwing will enable you to take advantage of a momentary lapse in balance to render a dangerous opponent helpless. This chapter discusses the basic skills you need to become an expert at *nage waza*.

Gripping (*kumikata*)

Top competitors understand how to dominate opponents and distract them from their match strategy. An important objective in combat is to bring the opponent into your area of relative strength, to fight on your terms. One way of doing this is through superior gripping skills. A contestant with a superior grip can attack freely, while preventing the opponent from doing so. Learn to strike like a hawk to grab your opponent so that he or she cannot block your attempt. Then throw immediately, or at least maintain the dominant grip so you have control over your opponent's movements.

In judo competition, or in a conflict off the mat, it is vital to control the space between you and your opponent. This is the area you have to manoeuvre through to get into a close position to attack—and your opponent has to travel through this same space to attack you. The primary tool you have to control that space is your grip.

Another purpose of gripping skill, or *kumikata*, is to provide the turning leverage usually needed to unbalance and throw an opponent. Grips along the opponent's center line are generally considered more defensive, whereas wider grips permit more attacks. For this reason, the most standard grip is one hand on the lapel at the chest and the other hand on the sleeve. This gives a balanced grip for optimal attack and defense. The pulling hand on the sleeve is called *hikite*, and the lifting or power hand at the lapel is called *tsurite*. For competition, practice your attacks from many different grips so you will be prepared to throw even when your favorite grip is not possible.

Kumikata provides the physical connection with your opponent that allows you to feel and anticipate an attack before it becomes a real threat. Because judo is a close-range form of fighting, reaction time must be extremely fast and visual cues are not very useful. You must learn to react to tactile stimuli, and your reactions must become reflexive. With training, your grip can give you valuable information about your opponent's actions early enough for you to respond. In addition to helping with your defense, your hands help you recognize when your opponent is in a vulnerable position so you can best apply your own throws. To gain these benefits, your arms must be relaxed so you can perceive subtle shifts in movement and balance. It is normal to try to throw your opponent after his balance is broken, but it is better to feel the opponent's intentions, anticipate his movements, and apply the throw at the same time as balance is broken.

In today's high-level competition, gripping skills have become a vital component of success. There are numerous tournament rules relating to how you can grip your opponent—intended to prevent defensive play and to

The left versus right grip is known as *kenka yotsu*.

ensure a fair fight. The most important rule is that you must obtain a normal grip. Normal *kumikata*, under the rules of competition, means taking hold of the left side of the opponent's jacket above the belt with the right hand, and the right side of the opponent's jacket above the belt with the left hand. You cannot grip the end of the sleeve at the opening, the belt, the pants, or grip with both hands on one side of your opponent, except when attacking. You also may not avoid gripping in order to prevent action.

As you train for your favorite throws, you must deal with two fundamental forms of *kumikata*. *Aiyotsu* is when both contestants take the same right- or left-handed grip (e.g. they both have their right hand on the opponent's lapel, with their left hand on the sleeve). *Kenka yotsu* is the non-symmetrical grip when a left-handed fighter meets a right-handed fighter (i.e. they engage one another using opposite grips).

In addition to these basic variations are many other forms of gripping that affect your ability to use your throws, including gripping the jacket over the back, behind the neck, around the waist, in the armpit, behind the shoulder, and gripping near the ends of both sleeves. As you train, learn to use the grip that maximizes your ability to throw, and to defend against dominant grips from your opponent.

Posture (*shisei*)

In most sports, a defensive posture is characterized by a low, bent-over position, while offensive posture is more upright. An offensive player with a football or basketball generally moves or stands with slightly bent legs while looking for an opportunity. The opposing defender has legs spread farther apart, assumes a more crouched position, and is focused on the ball. As soon as the defender gets the ball he stands up straighter to take the offensive —the standing position gives freedom of movement to change directions, use either foot, deceive opponents with feints, and see the entire competition area. In judo you cannot win without an effective attack, so the emphasis in practice is on the correct offensive posture.

The ideal posture to freely apply judo throws is an upright natural posture, with knees slightly bent, head centerd over the hips, feet directly below the hips and about shoulder width apart. Position your head so you look not down at your feet, but up around your opponent's waist or above. Movement of the hips will usually signal your opponent's real intentions better than his or her feet or hands, which often are used deceptively.

The ideal judo posture allows for free movement, and is inherently stable and balanced. The upright natural posture gives the best overall view of the field of battle, prevents you from being dominated, and allows you maximum freedom to react spontaneously when needed. The rules of competition penalize an overly defensive, bent-over position because it inhibits action.

The perfect technique is one without much effort or conscious thought, applied at the right time, in the right direction, with the right amount of force—a spontaneous reaction to the opportunity presented by the opponent's movement. This perfection is rare. In fact, technique is like water forever slipping through your fingers; the only expertise we can hope to develop is occasionally to remember to cup our hands. We can gather it together for a moment, sometimes long enough to take a refreshing drink, but it is too fluid to capture at will. The natural posture is therefore essential for the quick responses needed to take advantage of fleeting opportunities.

Learn from the mistakes of others; you may not live long enough to make them all yourself.

Good balance requires good posture.

Movement (*tai sabaki* and *shintai*)

Since judo requires you to maintain your own balance even in the face of a skilled opponent who is trying to knock you down, how you move your feet and your body is important. *Shintai* means "advance or retreat" and simply refers to the methods of walking used in judo.

The most useful method is *tsugi ashi*, which is often used in practice, particularly while learning a throw. In *tsugi ashi* (literally "next" or "following foot") you step with one foot then bring the other foot up to, but not past, the first without bringing them completely together. The feet should slide on the mat when stepping, with little or no lifting.

In tournaments or free practice your foot movements are crucial to maintaining a stable position. The easiest way for an opponent to throw you is to seize the opportunity while you move your feet before your body, or when you move them in an attempt to catch up with your body. Learn to keep your feet directly under your hips as much as possible. Crossing your feet, lifting them up, bringing them together or separating them too much can all lead to your being thrown. At the same time, being too predictable in your movement is dangerous too.

Knowledge of balance is the secret that enables masters of judo to throw stronger and heavier assailants without any great effort. It is the quick and agile person who has the ability to regain balance more easily, not the big, strong person, for strength is not a factor in balance. How well you move will be the determining factor in any conflict, whether you are strong or weak. To keep your movements natural and agile, avoid tension and rigidity in your body. Suppleness in your movement allows you to attack freely while retaining your balance and responding appropriately to your opponent's initiatives.

Tai sabaki, or body control, are the methods of turning used to defend yourself from throws, and to set up or enter for an attack of your own. The concept of *tai sabaki* is that the movement of the body, particularly the rotation of the body when it is upright, creates forces that can be used to help you evade throws, block throws, or effect throws. For example, by rotating your body in a small arc while holding your opponent, you can make your opponent move in a much larger arc around you. This allows you to maintain your own balance while creating the opportunity to take advantage of your opponent's greater movement.

Unbalancing (*kuzushi*)

The sense of balance is often taken for granted by athletes, overlooked as a skill worth attention and study. But mastery of balance is key to developing fighting skills. Jigoro Kano emphasized it as the key to success in judo.

Balance is controlled by a combination of three sensory inputs: the vestibular system in the inner ear, vision, and proprioception. Most people focus on vision as the primary tool to maintain balance, but in judo proprioception is vital. This is the kinesthetic perception of movement and spatial orientation arising from stimuli within the body itself. It is often more reliable than vision, and is the feel you get only from repeated practice. Balance involves a delicate interplay between forces to achieve a state of equilibrium or, conversely, a state of imbalance. The subtlety of your opponent's balance can often be detected only through your hands, which are in contact with your opponent.

Sometimes judo students are frustrated when they cannot easily apply throws on skilled training partners. As you progress, keep in mind that students who practice judo are probably the hardest people in the world to knock off their feet because they learn through painful experience what will happen to them if they lose their balance. They become expert in ways to retain control of their balance, or to regain it when it is in danger of being lost.

Although simple to understand in concept, *kuzushi* is difficult to achieve against a trained opponent who is conscious of his balance, who maintains good posture, and moves quickly with confidence. Against an attacker untrained in judo, the secrets of *kuzushi* will usually work easily to weaken his position so that he can be defeated. *Kuzushi* literally means "to destroy, demolish or break down." In judo it means to unbalance your opponent, or to break down his posture and destroy his stability. Its purpose is to force your opponent into a vulnerable position, one in which he or she cannot defend successfully. This can be a dynamic disruption of your opponent's balance, or it can be simply adapting to your opponent's movement. *Kuzushi* is attained when your opponent's center of gravity is not directly over his feet.

Success is going from failure to failure without losing your enthusiasm.

— *Winston Churchill*

There are three primary ways of applying *kuzushi*:
- your direct action (e.g. pulling or pushing as you enter for a throw);
- inducing your opponent's action (e.g. a feint or combination attack);
- direct action by your opponent (e.g. a counter throw).

Sometimes *kuzushi* is applied directly by simply pushing or pulling, which is how it is initially practiced as you are learning throws. Each hand has a specific role in bringing your opponent in the desired direction. The pushing or pulling motion is an integral part of each throw that must be strengthened and co-ordinated. You may eventually find that your own strength is sometimes insufficient to force your opponent's weight into a vulnerable position, and that your opponent can use his own muscles and weight to fight back.

Another way of directly applying *kuzushi* is by generating momentum from moving your body, then using this force to disrupt the balance of your opponent. Do this by moving your body quickly in the direction of the desired throw, building momentum the faster you move. Then transfer that momentum to your opponent's body when you bump into him or her, or reach the limit of your arm length. This sudden transfer of momentum, used for example in *osoto gari* (page 90), can result in a large and relatively effortless unbalancing force.

Because judo is a fluid activity with both contestants moving constantly, there are many opportunities for you to create and take advantage of momentary lapses in balance while shifting weight between the feet. *Kuzushi* achieved from one attempted throw can be used to attack with another follow-up throw. This is the basis for combination techniques that use the initial attack as a form of *kuzushi*. Alternatively, the shifting state of balance during your opponents' attacks can be used against them, and they can be thrown with counter throws.

As you become more advanced you learn to use your opponents' own efforts against them. If your opponent pulls you, try to advance with the pull to retain your balance, and add your own push to unbalance your opponent. Your opponent's strength can only be applied to you to the degree that you try to resist it. Without resistance, strength is meaningless. The idea is that you should push when pulled, and pull when pushed—the essence of yielding and the meaning of *ju*.

There are several ways that an opponent's movement can help you to apply *kuzushi* and achieve the state of imbalance that sets up a throw. If your opponent is moving forward, for example, and you stop his feet from moving while continuing the momentum of the upper body, his centre of gravity will naturally extend out in front of his feet so he can be toppled easily. An example of this type of *kuzushi* is seen in the throw *sasae tsuriko-mi ashi* (page 89).

Alternatively, if you simply stop or prevent the motion of your opponent's upper body while he is initiating a quick movement forward, he may complete the step he started and leave his center of gravity behind him so that you can throw him backwards with a throw such as *osoto gari* (page 90).

To create this kind of imbalance all you have to do is get the feet to move at a different speed than the upper body—either faster or slower. Since you can partially control the movement of the upper body through proper gripping (*kumikata*), you can influence your opponent's balance in almost undetectable ways as he moves his feet. You can also make him move his feet away from his center of gravity by applying foot sweeps, or making other attacks that cause him to move his feet, while controlling his upper body.

Another type of *kuzushi* based on the scientific principle of action-reaction is called *hando no kuzushi*, or reactionary breaking of balance. Using this principle you apply force to the opponent, but when you feel the typical response of resistance you reverse the direction to take advantage of the opponent's reaction. In this way every action or reaction of the opponent can be turned against him. Through constant practice you can anticipate certain reactions to your pushing or pulling, and then put yourself into a position to seize the opportunity you created through your action. Resistance often leads to defeat and it is sometimes better to resist with non-resistance.

To visualize the objective of *kuzushi*, imagine a large box representing an opponent (*see* diagram, right). While the box can be pushed backward or to one side (and many throws do exactly that), it is weakest when perched on one corner. This is the state often sought in judo so that a throw can be applied with the least amount of effort and strength. In this position the balance of the box is so precarious that it can be thrown in nearly any direction. In the case of a person who might try to move, this position also places all of his weight onto one part of one foot, making it difficult or impossible to move that foot to escape. Part of the benefit of *kuzushi* is that it often pins the opponent into a vulnerable

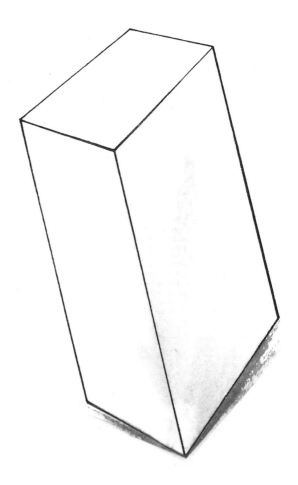

Think of this box as an opponent. It can be pushed backward or to one side and is weakest when perched on one corner. That is the principle of *kuzushi*.

position from which he cannot regain balance. This requires a finely tuned sense of balance and complete control over the opponent.

So how can you prevent an opponent from applying *kuzushi* to you? How should you deal with someone who attempts to pull you forward into a throw? If you resist by pulling back you may be thrown in that direction, but if you go forwards you may be in danger of falling right into a forward throw. The answer is to use the attacker's pull to throw him while keeping your own balance. To do this you can step forward faster and stronger than his pull required, so that you seize the initiative and unbalance him. By adding your own power and momentum to his pulling action, you can throw your opponent backwards. Another choice is to step diagonally forward and to one side, so that you go with the pull but redirect it into a new direction that forces the attacker off balance while preventing him from throwing you in the direction he was pulling.

There is also a form of mental *kuzushi* used to disturb your opponent psychologically or unbalance his or her composure and concentration. This can be achieved simply with a fighting spirit that dominates your opponent, use of the *kiai* (spirit shout) or physical manoeuvers that distract the opponent's attention away from your true objective. Gripping is very important as a means for controlling your opponent's focus of attention, as well as his posture and balance.

You can also sometimes create a mindset that can be used to defeat your opponent. For example, you can keep your opponent so mentally occupied in defending your attacks that he finds it difficult to initiate his own attacks. Certain attacks may be used simply to lure your opponent into a particular desired reaction. By constantly attacking with backward throws, you can create an almost unconscious reaction in your opponent, forcing him to maintain a posture with a slight forward push. Since the mind controls the body, you can often only apply *kuzushi* to an opponent who does not realize you are doing it.

Mastering *kuzushi* also means mentally training to prevent a sudden crisis from destroying your own demeanour. Judo training will help you to develop healthy reactions to a variety of confrontations. You will also develop a strong spirit, so that you can endure people who try to intimidate or bully you, while remaining focussed on your own specific objectives. Learning how to control your emotional reaction and rely on a calm inner self are part of maintaining the state of harmony that is balance.

Judo fundamentally revolves around the principle of balance. In fact, all things in life seek the balanced state, which is simply the unity of opposites. Life is the constant effort to elevate yourself while achieving and maintaining the harmonious state of balance from which you cannot fall. There can be no better training for this kind of life than judo.

Success is often nothing more than taking advantage of an opportunity given to you as a gift.

Learn to maintain a calm inner center in order to be able to weather the storm around you.

Fitting in (*tsukuri*)

A vital component of every throw is getting into the position needed to best apply the technique with minimal effort. Fitting in for the throw is called *tsukuri* (literally "to make"). It is closely linked with methods of *tai sabaki* and *kuzushi*, which often happen at the same time you are entering for a throw. While *kuzushi* is focused on your opponent's imbalance and weak position, *tsukuri* is focussed on your own balance while putting yourself into a position of strength. The object of *tsukuri* is to maintain your opponent's weak position while aligning your own body to take advantage of the opponent's loss of balance.

Tsukuri is the part of a throw practiced repeatedly in *uchikomi* so that the ideal throwing position can be attained quickly and spontaneously on demand. Appropriate emphasis should be made on creating and maintaining proper *kuzushi* during every practice of *tsukuri*. There are standard entries for basic throws, but also many individual variations for different body types, personal preferences, situations, and opportunities.

Through repetition you make the technique your own, adapt it to fit your particular preferences, and find out what works against different opponents. Stepping or pivoting into the correct foot position is a critical aspect of *tsukuri*. During these steps you are most vulnerable to a counter attack so they must be fast and accurate. It is especially important to master the rotating action needed for forward throws like *seoi nage*, shoulder throw. To apply this type of throw, you turn to face the same way as your opponent so he or she can be pulled onto or around your back. These turning actions are called *tai sabaki*, and the core concept is that you must continue breaking your opponent's balance by using the rotating action of your body in conjunction with your pulling. The pulling force should come more from the rotation and momentum of your body than the strength in your arms.

The most basic entry taught to beginners (Method 1 below) is to step forward with the right foot, placing it in front of the left foot, then to pivot on the ball of the right foot as you turn and bring the left foot back in line with the

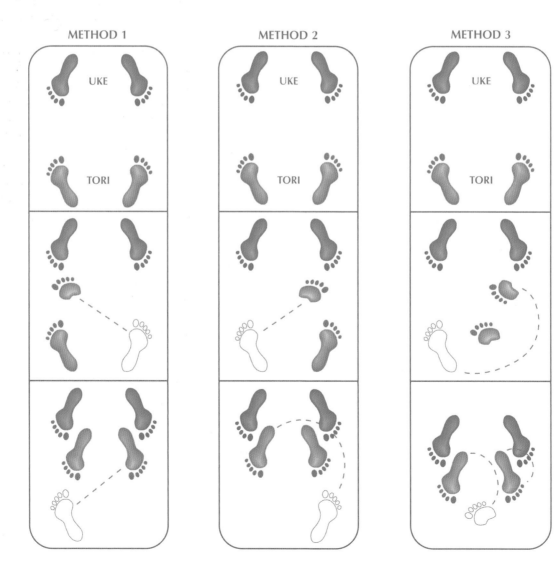

METHOD 1	METHOD 2	METHOD 3
UKE	UKE	UKE
TORI	TORI	TORI

right foot. Method 2 is to begin with the left foot, deceptively stepping in front of your right foot, then spinning in (*mawarikomi*) for the attack to the right side. Method 3, which is particularly fast and strong, is where the left foot steps first, behind the right foot. This type of rotation can be done while stepping backwards, pulling strongly with the left hand as you step away from your opponent to generate forward momentum. It is called drawing out (*hikidashi*). The fastest but most difficult method is to jump in with both feet at the same time as you turn in the air (*tobikomi*). The first three entry methods are shown in the illustrations on page 52. The person being thrown is called *uke*, while the person performing the throw is *tori*.

Turning or stepping to enter for a throw is an important part of *tsukuri*, but other critical elements include the position of your hands on your opponent, the exact alignment of your feet on the mat (or on the opponent), the direction of your push or pull with each hand, your body posture, and the position of your shoulders and head.

Application (*kake*)

The final phase of any throw is called *kake*—application of the technique. After breaking your opponent's balance so he is in a disadvantageous position (*kuzushi*), move your body into the most advantageous position for applying the technique (*tsukuri*), then execute it (*kake*). Think of *kuzushi* as disrupting an opponent's balance, and *kake* as making the state of imbalance decisive and permanent.

The *kake* in each technique is completed differently. You may bend, twist, sweep, push, fall, or roll to finish a throw. Often the application of a technique involves a complex movement of turning while leaning, pulling with the hands, and driving with the legs. Co-ordination of the various parts of the throw is an important skill; the more efficient it is, the more power and control you have.

A critical part of *kake* is the follow through. After your opponent starts to fall, you must maintain control and continue to execute the technique, following the opponent to the ground if necessary. Many skilled judo competitors can turn out to escape from a throw given even a minimal loss of contact or control by the thrower. Since the objective in competition is to ensure your opponent falls on his back with force and speed, your control of the opponent must be flawless and continuous until his back hits the ground (and even afterwards, to initiate groundwork while still in an advantageous position). In modern competition this type of approach is called terminal judo, because when the proper angle of attack is utilized with good follow through, every throw will end with both contestants driven onto the mat with force.

Combination techniques (*renraku waza*)

Judo is not as simple as memorizing the various techniques and how to apply them. If it were that easy, there would be many more black belts. The problem when trying to apply your favourite throw successfully is that your opponent never stands still. As you improve your technique, your opponent is often improving his defences. This means you have to learn ways to force or coax your opponent into a position of vulnerability, and immediately take advantage of the opportunity created.

Before you can expect to be successful with combination techniques you need to master the basic throws and common defenses. However, combinations are essential for intermediate and advanced students, who often have difficulty with single attacks against equally skilled opponents or with defensive opponents who are ready to apply a counter throw.

Any good attempt at a throw should at least make your opponent lose balance and become vulnerable to a subsequent attack. In the fleeting moments while he or she is regaining balance, you should be spontaneously attacking with a combination throw, or *renraku waza*. Naturally, the technique used to set up your primary attack, or to follow up your initial unsuccessful attack, must be appropriate to the situation. This requires careful planning and training on transitions between throws, taking into account the likely reactions of your opponent.

When you repeatedly attack with certain throws your opponent's response eventually becomes predictable. Each attempted throw generally results in specific evasions, blocks, and counter attacks from your opponent. When you see this happening, it is time to prepare for your opponent's response and continue directly into another attack. Sometimes a string of multiple attacks is planned to force your opponent off balance. Later, when you can better predict your opponent's movement, you may be able to use a feint to fake an attack that results in a desired reaction from your opponent. Basically, you learn to draw out the movement you want from your opponent by using combinations to create opportunities. This is an active form of breaking balance, or *kuzushi*.

One type of combination attack is to continue directly from a throwing attempt into a technique on the ground, such as an arm lock or a pin. A common example is *tai otoshi* (body drop—page 74) followed by *juji gatame* (cross arm lock—page 142). Once on the ground you should continue to be flexible in your attacks, moving fluidly from one attack to another. Sometimes as your opponent begins to escape from your pin you can switch to another pin, or achieve a submission by choke or arm lock. Yielding to superior strength may lead to other openings, whereas rigidly sticking with a weak position usually leads to defeat.

To succeed with combination techniques, your transition from one throw to another must be seamless and quick. Your training should include practice on combinations for your favorite throws so you can perform them naturally, without thinking. Preparations you make today will help you win tomorrow. There are many *renraku waza* that can be used in various situations to throw your opponent. For a comprehensive list *see* pages 149–151.

Counter techniques (*kaeshi waza*)

When you are attacked, your opponent gives you a present of his strength. You must know how to receive it and turn it to your advantage. Counter techniques, or *kaeshi waza*, rely on an opponent's attack to create the momentum and *kuzushi* for your own attack. Counter techniques are risky in that you must allow your opponent to take the initiative, so they require confidence that you can successfully resist being thrown. Specialists in *kaeshi waza* find, however, that when they are prepared for an attack it is easier to take advantage of an opponent than when he is not moving. Every attempted attack creates certain vulnerabilities that can be exploited—if you can retain your own balance.

The best way to retain your balance and prepare for a counterattack is to spoil the key element that makes your opponent's attempted throw work. To do this, you must thoroughly understand the principles of each throw that you want to counter. You can then react to each throw with the exact movement required to stop it. You can also deceptively create an apparent opportunity for your opponent to attack, knowing that when he does you are ready with a counter. For example, you may leave one foot in front of the other, encouraging your opponent to see it as an opportunity for a foot sweep, while you are prepared to counter the sweep when it comes.

One thing you learn very well in judo is that every attack has an appropriate defense. One of the earliest westerners to witness judo in the 19th century was the American writer Lafcadio Hearn, who wrote:

I may venture to say, loosely, that in judo there is a sort of counter for every twist, wrench, pull, push, or bend. Only the judo expert does not oppose such movements at all. No, he yields to them. But he does much more than yield to them. He aids them with a wicked sleight that causes the assailant to put out his own shoulder, to fracture his own arm, or in a desperate case, even to break his own neck or back.

Throws are not isolated moves; they are always performed in a fluid combat situation. As you attack, your opponent may respond with his or her own counterattack, and you must in turn respond with your combination technique. As you learn combination and counter techniques the lines will begin to blur between attack and defense. In fact, one of the paradoxes of judo is that offense is defense, defense is offense.

To succeed, your reaction to your opponent's attacks must be swift and instinctive. Your training must include practice on both the basic technique and the counters for it, so that you know them intimately. The ability to win a match or save your life in an attack comes only from diligent preparation. Many *kaeshi waza* can be used in various situations to throw your opponent, and a list of suggested techniques is provided on pages 149–151.

Attack initiative (*sen*)

Judo is a subtle and sublime art. As important as the physical aspects of judo are, it is also mentally stimulating—one reason it is considered an educational system. Students often spend considerable time and energy figuring out how to make a technique work correctly, understanding why the opponent's technique could not be avoided, and developing strategies for success.

One key strategy worth in-depth investigation involves the interplay between attack and defense. We have all heard the saying that the best defense is a good offense. In judo it is generally accepted that the key to success is to strike before your opponent has the opportunity to win. Since judo matches end when one point is achieved, there are no second chances. This teaches you to be decisive, to respond to attacks with your own attacks, and whenever possible to pre-empt your opponent's attacks to prevent them from being successful.

Jigoro Kano recognized three different levels of combative initiative, or *sen*:
• *Go no sen* is the form of attack we normally think of as a counterattack. By taking advantage of the opponent's movement and position after he or she has started the attack, this form of attack initiative is considered a late

Sense your opponent's intentions by feeling them with your hands.

form of initiative. It is usually characterized as a defensive response, or counteraction to an unsuccessful attack attempted by your opponent.

• *Sen* is the form of attack initiative that is also defensive, but launched simultaneously with the aggressor's attack. This requires a definitive understanding of the form the attack will take, based on the initial move or preparation leading up to the attack.

• *Sen-sen no sen* is a subconscious form of attack initiative that is also defensive, but appears to be offensive. The aggressor's attack is anticipated and "beaten to the punch" by an appropriate action. This requires that you should recognize your opponent's intent even before the attack has been launched.

Through your practice of judo you will learn to feel your opponent's intentions the moment he or she starts to focus on an attack. It has been said that the arms are but an extension of the mind. In judo practice you are directly connected to your opponent through the arms, and it is not unusual to sense the same things as your opponent. By being aware of your opponent's grip, posture, focus, tension, movements, and so on, you can tell much about what your opponent will do next. In ice hockey they say, "Skate to where the puck is going and not to where it has been." In judo, the only way to get ahead of the game is to heighten your ability to perceive your opponent's intentions. To do this, your mind must be relaxed and receptive, your body fluid to respond with utmost quickness to each threat. Even if you know your opponent's intentions, your conscious mind may not be able to formulate a response and direct your body to perform it in time. Both the perception of your opponent's attack and your response must be instinctive. To achieve this requires repetitive physical training, but developing a certain mental awareness is also necessary. Cultivate a mental state like a calm mountain pond, reflecting all that is around it. In Japanese this is called *mizu no kokoro* (mind like water) or *mushin* (no-mind). Your awareness can become as immediate, and your actions as instantaneous, as the moon, which is infinitely far away yet loses no time revealing its reflection on the water as soon as the clouds break.

Unlike a calm pond, judo can be a tumultuous, dynamic activity that is far from meditative. To deal with the chaos of combat, *samurai* warriors were trained to develop a combative mental state of *fudo shin* (immovable mind). This state of awareness is equated with the moon reflected in a stream: though the waters are in motion around it, the moon retains its serenity. In judo combat you move in spontaneous response to the turbulence of each situation, but your mental state should remain the same—determined and master of the self.

Hip throws (koshi waza)

The hips (pelvis) provide the power for all hip throws. If you use them as the fulcrum of a large lever, placing them lower than your opponent's center of gravity, his upper body weight will make him tumble over you. Using your hips helps you topple opponents larger than you, using their forward momentum or weight against them.

Most, but not all, hip throws are done in a forward direction—the direction your opponent is advancing. All techniques are described to the right side, but you must also practice the left-side version.

There are many effective ways to perform these techniques under different conditions. The techniques described in this and subsequent chapters are the most basic and standard versions, generally those taught by the Kodokan and demonstrated in promotional examinations. Some non-standard grips and applications of these techniques are shown to demonstrate alternatives. Modifications can be made for tournaments or self-defense, and we will look at some suggestions on how to do this.

Some follow-up moves and counterattacks are suggested in this and subsequent chapters to give an idea of the possibilities, but a full list can be found on pages 149–151.

UKI GOSHI (floating hip throw)

The favorite throw of Jigoro Kano, this throw is one of the easiest to apply as a beginner. While effective against an untrained opponent, it is quite easily avoided by a knowledgeable adversary and seldom seen in tournaments. It is usually applied to an opponent (*uke*) who is advancing or pushing forwards.

Key points:

- Your right hand grabs around the waist and pulls *uke* very tightly to your own right hip, as your left hand pulls around you.
- By twisting your upper body, *uke* will rotate around your hips. Additional forward pull is created when you shift your weight from your right foot to your left foot, pulling *uke* off his feet and onto your hip as you do so.
- Do not bend over or lift with the legs in *uki goshi*; twist to your left to generate the power of the throw.

To prevent your opponent from applying *uki goshi* to you, step around with your right foot to avoid hip contact, or bend the knees to squat low. Counter with *ushiro goshi* (page 66), *utsuri goshi* (page 67), *tani otoshi* (page 105), or *sukui nage* (page 76).

If *uki goshi* does not work, follow up with another throw like *harai goshi* (page 64) or *kouchi gari* (if your opponent steps around your hip—page 95), or *o goshi* (if your opponent bends the knees to get low—page 59).

UKE

TORI

Left: A typical foot position for the person being thrown (*uke*) is represented by the blue color. The basic foot position for the person performing the throw (*tori*) is grey. These positions can vary considerably. Note that only right-side throws are shown.

O GOSHI (large hip throw)

O goshi is similar to *uki goshi* (page 58) except the legs are used to lift *uke* up and over your hips, rather than twisting *uke* around your hips.

Key points:

- Your hip in *o goshi* is placed a little further in front of *uke* than in the previous throw.
- To apply the lifting action your feet must be close together, with the knees bent, so your hips are under your opponent's.
- When you are ready to throw, pull with your hands, straighten your legs, lifting *uke* off the ground; bend forward slightly and twist your upper body to the left.

If your opponent comes around your hip to escape your attack, you can try *o goshi* again, or follow up with *harai goshi* (page 64) or *kouchi gari* (page 95). If your opponent pulls back, switch to *ouchi gari* (page 92).

You can counter an adversary who is applying *o goshi* to you with *ushiro goshi* (page 66), *utsuri goshi* (page 67), *tani otoshi* (page 105), or *sukui nage* (page 76). You may also block *o goshi*, or any forward hip or shoulder throw, with a hip smash. To accomplish this, thrust your left hip forward to meet your opponent's attacking right hip, twist your upper body and hips to your right, step your right foot back if possible, and yank your right arm back in the direction you are turning. The stronger you twist and pull backwards with your right arm, the stronger your left hip will smash into your attacker's hip, helping you retain your balance while upsetting your attacker's.

Close-up

Self-defense variation with arm bar

TSURI GOSHI (lifting hip throw)

Tsuri goshi is similar to the preceding hip throws, except that you grab the belt with your hand and pull *uke* up onto your hip. There are two versions: *o tsuri goshi* (big lifting hip throw) and *ko tsuri goshi* (small lifting hip throw). In *o tsuri goshi* you reach over *uke*'s arm to grab the belt, trapping *uke*'s arm; in *ko tsuri goshi* you grab the belt after reaching under *uke*'s arm.

The foot position is generally the same as *o goshi*, but it can be done more sideways, with less rotation of your hips, so the entry can be quicker.

Key points:

- Lift *uke* strongly with the combined power of your hand lifting *uke*'s belt and your hips rising under *uke*.
- Try to get a grip on the belt before starting to attack.
- *Uke* should be off balance forward, but with a strong pull you can often defeat even a resisting opponent.

If *tsuri goshi* does not work, follow up with *harai goshi* (page 64) or *ouchi gari* (page 92). *O tsuri goshi* is an effective counter for the opposite side attack from *ko tsuri goshi*, and vice versa

Close-up

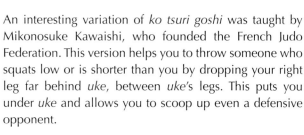

An interesting variation of *ko tsuri goshi* was taught by Mikonosuke Kawaishi, who founded the French Judo Federation. This version helps you to throw someone who squats low or is shorter than you by dropping your right leg far behind *uke*, between *uke*'s legs. This puts you under *uke* and allows you to scoop up even a defensive opponent.

Variation: *ko tsuri goshi*

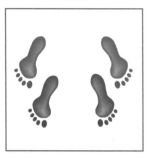

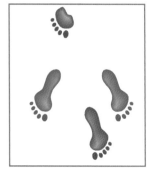

KOSHI GURUMA (hip wheel)

In this throw you lower your hip and roll *uke* over it like a large wheel. The centre, or hub, of the wheel is your hip, while your arms and legs are the spokes. The basic position is similar to *o goshi*, but instead of placing your hand around *uke*'s waist, you place it behind the head or around the neck and use it to pull *uke* forward. Usually this hand is not gripping the jacket while throwing, so *koshi guruma* works better against an opponent whose head is up, rather than someone who is bent over and looking down. The hip position for *koshi guruma* is typically deeper than *o goshi*, and the foot position may be turned slightly more, as shown.

Key points:

- Pull *uke* forward with your left hand as you slip your right hand far around *uke*'s neck.
- Bring your hip very far in front of *uke*.
- Continue rotating to your left and pull *uke* over you.

TSURIKOMI GOSHI (lifting pulling hip throw)

Tsurikomi goshi, as it is known today, was created by Jigoro Kano in response to an opponent who stiffened up straight and pulled back to prevent *uki goshi* (page 58) or *o goshi* (page 59). In *tsurikomi goshi* you drop very low so your hips make contact on uke's thighs, increasing the leverage available to throw *uke*. To increase the leverage even further, maintain your right-hand grip high on *uke*'s lapel. *Uke* feels like a stiff tree being toppled by the wind.

In competition or free practice, *tsurikomi goshi* may also be performed in a higher version called *taka tsurikomi goshi*, using the same hip position as *o goshi*. This allows you to use a hip throw to attack without changing your grip since you are already hanging on to the lapel. The foot position for any *tsurikomi goshi* is the same as *o goshi*.

Key points:

- The right hand pulls towards the thumb, while the opposite side of your hand and forearm are against the left side of *uke*'s chest.
- Do not let your right hand get behind your own head and shoulders or it will lose its strength.
- Drop as low as you can by bending the knees once you feel *uke* is off balance forwards. If *uke* is sufficiently off balance you should not feel much weight on you when you throw.

Close-up

Variation: *taka tsurikomi goshi*

SODE TSURIKOMI GOSHI
(sleeve lifting pulling hip throw)

This variation can help you to throw your opponent if you have difficulty getting low enough to apply the regular *tsurikomi goshi* (page 62). Switch your right-hand grip from *uke's* lapel to *uke's* left sleeve at the elbow. When you drive uke's left elbow high into the air, you increase the leverage on *uke*, reducing the need to get your hips low. This throw may be used when *uke* is stiff-arming you to keep you away; since you lift strongly on the elbow you can break *uke's* defensive grip.

Key points:

- Grab *uke's* left sleeve at the elbow with your palm up and fingers pointing to the outside.
- Lift *uke's* left elbow as high as possible, placing your right elbow into *uke's* armpit.
- Place your right hip in deeply as you lift and pull *uke* over you.

HARAI GOSHI (sweeping hip throw)

One defence for *tsurikomi goshi* (page 62) is to step around or over your attacker's hip. *Harai goshi* is used to prevent this escape. This is the third hip throw performed in the *nage no kata*, but the first where you stand on one foot. It is a powerful throw often used in tournaments.

Uke is generally advancing or leaning towards his or her right front when *harai goshi* is applied, but it is a versatile throw that can be used when uke is moving in any direction. You can maintain a normal grip (left hand on the sleeve and right hand on the lapel of uke), you can grab the collar behind the neck, or you can grab around the back. Pull *uke*'s right arm with determination so that *uke* puts most of his weight onto the right foot. As you enter for *harai goshi* you will continue this pull so that *uke* leans even further over the toes of the right foot.

You enter for this throw so you are supporting yourself on your left leg with your foot between *uke*'s feet. Maintaining your balance on one leg is critical. Your right leg reaches across in front of *uke* to prevent *uke* from coming around your hip. Using your leg in a swinging motion, you sweep *uke*'s right leg out from under him.

Key points:

- Do not attempt a sweep until *uke* is off balance, well over his right foot.
- Keep *uke*'s body tightly against yours from your lower leg all the way to your right hand by continuing a strong pull around you with your left hand.
- As your foot and leg sweep up, your head and arms go down (along with *uke*).

Harai goshi can be combined easily with *osoto gari* (page 90) if your opponent changes directions. It can be blocked with the hip smash (*see* page 59) or countered with *ushiro goshi* (page 66), *utsuri goshi* (page 67), *ura nage* (page 108), *harai goshi gaeshi* (page 101), or *sukui nage* (*te guruma*, page 76).

▲ **Close-up**

HANE GOSHI (spring hip throw)

Hane goshi was developed by Yoshitsugu Yamashita (10th dan) around 1919 when he could no longer do his favourite technique, *harai goshi*. Although knee injury prevented him from stretching his leg across his opponent's, with his leg bent he could still lift his partner into the air.

The *kuzushi* for *hane goshi* is towards *uke*'s front and slightly to the right so that uke is advancing onto the right foot. The entry for *hane goshi* is similar to *harai goshi* (opposite) except you do not turn quite as far in, maintaining more of your side in contact with *uke*'s front. Your sweeping leg is bent a little so your knee is outside of *uke*'s leg, but your foot is between *uke*'s legs. As you twist to your left, pulling *uke*, lean forward, bringing *uke* with you because of the tight contact, while your right leg raises *uke*'s right leg.

Key points:

- The outside of your right leg contacts the inside of *uke*'s right leg.
- Point your toes down.
- Keep *uke*'s chest and abdomen tight against your side by pulling with both hands.

If *hane goshi* does not work because your opponent pulls back, your leg is in an excellent position to apply *ouchi gari* (page 92) to throw *uke* to the rear, or if *uke* is off balance forward, use *uchi mata* (page 96). The primary counterattack for *hane goshi* is *hane goshi gaeshi* (page 101), but *ushiro goshi* (page 66), *utsuri goshi* (page 67), *ura nage* (page 108), or *sukui nage* (*te guruma*, page 76) may also be used.

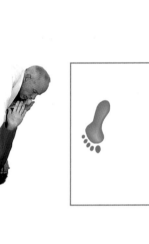

DAKI AGE (high lift)

This throw is used when *uke* is on his back with legs around your waist (guard position). Grab *uke*'s lapels, belt, or arms, lift *uke* high into the air, and slam *uke* onto his back. It is an excellent self-defense technique, but should not be used in free practice because of the risk of injury—*uke* may fall high on the upper back or neck, and *uke*'s head may hit the ground hard. Until the 1970s, judo competition rules awarded *ippon* (one point) for lifting an opponent to shoulder height, preventing the need for slamming or dropping *uke* to earn a score. Now it is considered too dangerous and is not permitted in competition. The referee stops a match as soon as you lift *uke* off the ground.

Key points:

- Keep *uke*'s hips close to you.
- Squat low to use your legs rather than your back to lift.
- Thrust your hips forward to aid your lifting action.

To defend against this throw, *uke* releases the legs around the waist as soon as *tori* starts to lift. *Uke* may also be able to grab *tori*'s ankles and push with the legs to force *tori* to fall backwards before *uke* is lifted too high.

USHIRO GOSHI (back hip throw)

This is a reversal used against an opponent who attempts a hip or shoulder throw on you. When *uke* enters for a throw like *o goshi* (page 59), bend your knees to drop your hips lower than *uke* and pull *uke* tightly against your chest and stomach. Lift *uke* by straightening your legs as you thrust your hips forward and lean backwards. *Uke* should feel like a large wave has come in from behind, sweeping out *uke*'s legs and floating *uke* onto the crest of the wave. Throw *uke* by stepping backwards with your left foot and dropping *uke* in front of you.

Key points:

- Spoil your opponent's attack first by sinking low; then perform the counter-throw.
- Hold *uke* tightly against your body.
- Lift *uke* as high as possible using strong hip action.

When *ushiro goshi* does not work, follow it up with *utsuri goshi* (page 67) or *ura nage* (page 108). If someone is attempting this throw on you, counter with an effective *sukui nage* (page 76) or *kosoto gari* (page 96).

UTSURI GOSHI (hip shift)

This throw begins with the same lifting action as *ushiro goshi* (opposite), but the throwing action is different. Instead of stepping back to finish the throw, step forward so *uke* will fall onto your hip and you can finish with a hip throw like *o goshi* (page 59). Sometimes *harai goshi* (page 64) is used to finish the throw instead. *Utsuri goshi* is particularly useful when the *ushiro goshi* is weak, and *uke*'s legs continue to hang down in such a way that they would land on the mat, making it difficult for you to throw *uke* onto his back. In *utsuri goshi*, *uke* is lifted into the air face up, then flipped completely over in one complete turn to land on the mat face up again.

Key points:

- Hold *uke* tightly to your body with your arms.
- Bend your knees to get under *uke* so you can lift *uke* high on your chest.
- Before *uke*'s feet come down on the ground, move your hip into position for the final hip throw.

Hand throws (te waza)

All throws involve nearly every part of the body acting in a co-ordinated manner. Hand throws are no exception, although the emphasis here is the action of the hands, arms, and shoulders. In some cases only the hands make contact with the opponent, while in other cases your hip or leg will help the throw by blocking *uke*.

The beauty of hand throws is that you can react quickly to take advantage of any weakness in *uke*'s balance while still transferring the power of your entire body into the throw. Your hands should always be in contact with your opponent, providing the means to upset his balance in very subtle – or quite dramatic – ways. Your arms may simply pull to encourage *uke* to move, or push to shift *uke*'s weight. In other throws, you may use your arms to turn, lift, trip, or roll *uke*. For success in *te waza*, focus on the effective use of your hands, arms, and shoulders without neglecting proper body mechanics or your opponent's movement.

SEOI NAGE (shoulder throw)

Seoi nage (also called *morote seoi nage*) is one of the most common and successful throws seen in tournaments. It is a favourite technique of Japanese female superstar Ryoko Tani, who used it successfully while dominating the under-48kg weight class to win six World Championship titles and two Olympic gold medals from 1993 to 2004.

It can be applied in a number of ways and has many variations. The basic idea is to start with a normal grip, turn so that *uke* is pulled onto your back, then bend forward and throw *uke* off your back to the ground. Apply this technique when *uke* is pushing or leaning forward.

Key points:

- Turn the right hand into the lapel so it is not bent backwards.
- Bend your knees to get as low as possible.
- As you throw, rotate your shoulders to the left, pulling *uke* over you. Turn your head to the left and bring your hands toward your left knee as you rotate.

Many other specialized versions of *seoi nage* use variations of the basic hand or foot position. In a version called *eri seoi nage*, the right hand grabs *uke*'s right lapel instead of the left. In tournaments *hantaigawa no seoi nage*, or inside-out shoulder throw, is applied to *uke*'s opposite arm. *Seoi nage* may also use different foot positions. Sometimes your right leg is used to block *uke*'s advancing right foot, similar to the foot position for *tai otoshi* (page 74). Alternatively, you can place your right foot deeper between *uke*'s legs, or with one or both knees on the ground. In each case, what makes it *seoi nage* is that it is a lifting throw where *uke* is picked up onto your back.

Seoi nage is combined effectively with backward throws since that is the direction *uke* will generally resist. *Ouchi gari* (page 92) and *kouchi gari* (page 95) are excellent preparatory or follow-up attacks. This throw may be countered with *ushiro goshi* (page 66), or *ura nage* (page 108).

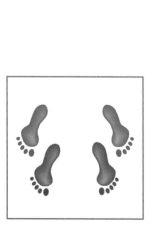

Variation: *hantai gawa no seoi nage*

Variation: drop-knee *seoi nage*

IPPON SEOI NAGE (one-arm shoulder throw)

This version of *seoi nage* is performed in *Nage no Kata* in response to an overhead blow. A popular tournament technique, is it also important for self-defense since it can be done without a *judogi* in response to a variety of attacks, and can be used to break the arm if necessary.

Key points:

• Start the *kuzushi* with a good pull from your left hand upward and forward, then enter and place *uke*'s arm well below the point of your own shoulder. Place your right arm tight into *uke*'s armpit so the back of your shoulder and upper back are in close contact with *uke*'s front.

• Bend your legs to get as low as possible so you can hoist *uke* onto your back.

• As you throw, pull both hands down and to your left to pull *uke* over you. Turn your head to the left and bring your hands towards your left knee as you rotate your upper body.

Close-up

One unorthodox way of performing *ippon seoi nage* is to apply the right-sided throw attacking *uke*'s left arm. It may also be performed against both of *uke*'s arms by gripping both sleeves.

If you miss the throw and go completely under *uke*'s arm, turn in for a *morote gari* (page 82). If *uke* resists backwards, attack with *osoto gari* (page 90) or *kouchi gari* (page 95).

Ippon seoi nage may be countered with *tani otoshi* (page 105), *ushiro goshi* (page 66) or *ura nage* (page 108).

Self-defense version with arm bar

Inside-out variation

Two-handed variation

TAI OTOSHI (body drop)

In this throw you pull *uke* off balance as *uke* is stepping forward with the right foot. Your right leg blocks *uke*'s advancing foot and *uke*'s upper body is pulled forward, then rotated down to the ground. *Tai otoshi* may sometimes be done more towards the right side if *uke* is moving in that direction. Because it is performed entirely with the hands, but without hip contact, using *uke*'s momentum is essential.

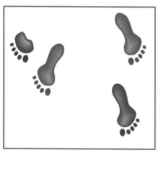

Key points:

- Spread your legs far apart for a stable base, with more of your weight on your left leg.
- Block *uke*'s right leg below the knee with your right leg so *uke*'s weight can come forward over his foot. Your right leg should be bent slightly before you apply the throw.
- Pull around you with your left hand and push with your right hand to rotate *uke*'s body, then twist your upper body and turn your head to the left.

Tai otoshi is often used in combination with *uchi mata* (page 96) or *ouchi gari* (page 92). If *uke* escapes your attempt by stepping over your leg, apply *tai otoshi* again. One way to counter it is to step over the attacking leg and apply *kouchi gari* (page 95).

KATA GURUMA (shoulder wheel)

Jigoro Kano learned this technique while studying Tenshin Shinyo Ryu Jujutsu as a young man. One of the advanced students was Fukushima, a large man Kano could not throw no matter how hard he tried, so he researched other methods to gain an advantage. He adapted a throw from wrestling to devise *kata guruma*, eventually using it to throw the mighty Fukushima. It is now included in the *Nage no Kata*.

The traditional way to perform *kata guruma* is to pull *uke* continuously forward with your left hand while you drop under *uke* and grab *uke*'s right leg with your right arm. *Uke* should be pulled onto your shoulders so you can stand up and throw *uke* down. The throw can also be performed on one or both knees between *uke*'s legs.

In competition it is also seen in a version that is more like a sacrifice throw: your left leg slides onto the mat in front of *uke*'s right foot and your left hip comes to the ground under *uke*. *Uke* is thrown to his right front corner as you fall onto the left side.

Key points:

- For maximum leverage and balance try to place *uke*'s waist directly behind your neck.
- Sink low and rise up as *uke*'s weight falls onto your shoulders. Keep your back straight up and use your legs to lift.
- Continue pulling with your left hand throughout the throw.

KATA GURUMA

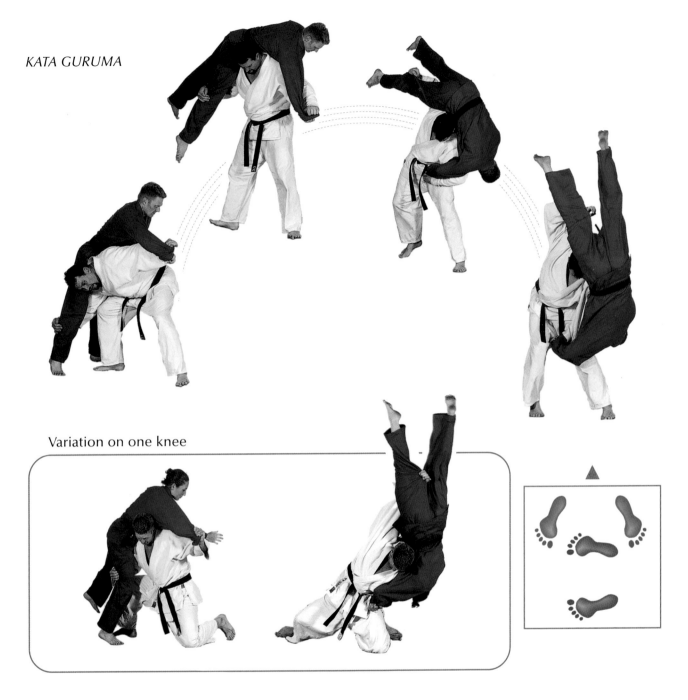

Variation on one knee

Variation as a sacrifice throw

SUKUI NAGE (scooping throw)

This is usually applied as a counter to a hip throw, or when your opponent has one foot well in front of the other. After you get behind *uke*, scoop out *uke*'s legs and throw *uke* over your leg directly onto his back.

Key points:

- Bend your right leg at almost a 90-degree angle so *uke* can fall over it.
- Grab both legs securely with your hands and hang on until *uke* is on the floor.
- Push *uke* backwards with your hips and shoulder as you scoop the legs.

Sometimes to make this throw work you will fall with *uke* as if it was a sacrifice throw. Another throw commonly called *te guruma* (*see* right) is considered by the Kodokan to be a variation of *sukui nage*. In this version, *uke* is lifted off the mats with the hips, then turned over with the hands.

Variation: *te guruma* (hand wheel)

This version of *sukui nage* was used by Robert van de Walle to win the gold medal match at the 1980 Olympics. As a counter throw, it is an ever-present threat to *osoto gari, harai goshi,* and *uchi mata,* demonstrating the significant power that can be generated if you anticipate an attack and harmonize with *uke*'s movement.

OBI OTOSHI (belt drop)

This is similar to *sukui nage* (page 76) in the foot position and the direction you throw your opponent (backward). However, the hand position is different and you can sometimes achieve a better lifting action. Grab the front of *uke*'s belt with your left hand, palm up, then reach across *uke*'s body with your right hand to grab the opposite arm, hip, or upper thigh.

Key points:

- Pull strongly with the hand on the belt to force *uke* to lean backwards to regain balance.
- Take advantage of the opportunity by entering quickly.
- Straighten your legs and push your hips forward as you lift *uke*.

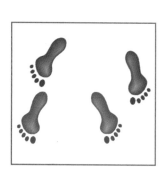

SUMI OTOSHI (corner drop)

This is similar to *uki otoshi* (opposite) since both are sometimes called air throws; here, however, the angle of attack is to *uke*'s right rear instead of forward. This throw is usually performed when *uke* is stepping forward or turning so that *uke*'s weight is on the right heel. Advance strongly with your left foot, as you would for *osoto gari* (page 90), and throw with a rotating motion of your arms.

Key points:

- Use this throw when *uke* is advancing and you have a chance to rapidly reverse *uke*'s motion in a circular fashion.
- Pull out and down sharply with your left hand on *uke*'s sleeve as you step forward with your left foot.
- Use your right hand first to pull, then to push *uke* down to the mat.

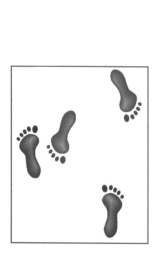

UKI OTOSHI (floating drop)

The first throw in the *Nage no Kata*, this is the classic demonstration of a hand throw since no other part of your body comes in contact with *uke*. It can be performed either on one knee, as it is in the *Nage no Kata*, or from a standing position.

Key points:

- Use this throw when *uke* is advancing and you have the opportunity to quickly extend *uke*'s center of gravity beyond his feet. Utilize *uke*'s momentum.
- Continue to pull *uke* forward, then pull down sharply with your left hand on the sleeve as you step back with your left foot and drop down onto your left knee.
- Pull *uke* past you with your right hand, then rotate *uke* down to the mat.

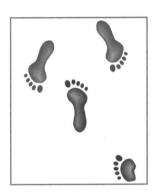

Standing variation

SEOI OTOSHI (shoulder drop)

This is similar to *seoi nage* (page 70) except that *uke* is not lifted up and over your shoulder, but dropped straight down. *Otoshi* means to let fall, so you must get low under *uke*. It relies on your dropping action to generate power. It can employ any of the hand positions used in *seoi nage*. *Tori* drops to one knee between *uke*'s legs (*see* foot diagram) or blocks *uke*'s leg as shown in the photographs.

Key points:

- Pull *uke* forward or take advantage of *uke*'s forward push.
- As you drop down pull *uke* with you, utilizing your body weight.
- Be careful to protect *uke*'s head from hitting the ground.

YAMA ARASHI (mountain storm)

Shiro Saigo, one of the four Heavenly Lords of early judo, made this throw famous, using it to win against early *jujutsu* masters in a tournament that led to the adoption of judo training by the Tokyo Metropolitan Police. It uses a whipping action, rotating *uke* around your base like the tempestuous winds of a mountain storm. Grab the top of *uke*'s right sleeve with both hands (*see* close-up), or grab *uke*'s right lapel with your right hand, thumb inside. Place your right foot across *uke*'s right leg, around the knee.

Key points:

- Grip securely with both hands on *uke*'s right sleeve or shoulder.
- Rotate *uke* around you with the pull of both hands.
- Block *uke* from advancing with your right leg.

Close-up

MOROTE GARI (two-hand reap)

In wrestling, this throw is called a double-leg takedown. *Uke*'s legs are grabbed and pulled out as *uke* falls backwards. You can use a powerful forward drive, a sharp lifting action, or both. You can reap *uke*'s legs out to the front or to the side.

Key points:

- Your hands should grab around *uke*'s legs as far and as tightly as possible.
- Push with your shoulder into *uke*'s body, and keep your head up.
- Lift and reap the legs by strongly pulling them out from under *uke* in the opposite direction from where you are pushing.

Lifting variation, sweeping legs to the side

KIBISU GAESHI (heel trip)

Deceptively simple, but very effective, this move is generally applied to *uke's* forward leg when *uke* is advancing.

Key points:

- As *uke* steps forward with the right foot, pull *uke's* weight strongly to your left with your left hand.
- Drop down quickly and grab *uke's* heel with your right hand.
- Continue the pull to your left as you lift the heel.

Close-up

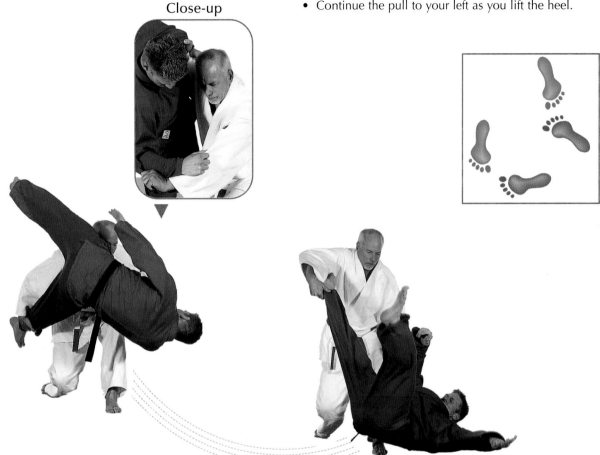

Combination: throwing with *kibisu gaeshi* after your opponent evades your *seoi otoshi* attack

KOUCHI GAESHI (small inner-reaping throw)
This is a counter throw used against an opponent who tries *kouchi gari* (page 95). As *uke* enters for *kouchi gari* against your right foot, lift your foot to escape, step back and twist to your right, throwing *uke* in front of you. Instead of stepping back you could also place your escaping right foot on *uke*'s left knee and apply *hiza guruma* (*see* box, bottom). The most basic method of *kouchi gaeshi* is to step back with your left foot, turn to the left, and throw *uke* (as shown below).

Key points:
• Maintain your balance while turning sharply.
• Take control of *uke*'s attack initiative.
• Rotate *uke*'s upper body as you twist to the side.

Hiza guruma version

KUCHIKI TAOSHI (one-hand or dead-tree drop)

Step deeply between *uke*'s legs with your right foot, reaching down with your left hand to grab *uke*'s right leg. Lift the leg as you drive *uke* backward with your body and right hand. This throw can be applied in combination with *kouchi gari* (page 95) or *ouchi gari* (page 92).

Key points:

- Use this technique when *uke* is straight, not bent over.
- Grab *uke*'s leg with as much of your arm as possible, and lift it high quickly.
- Drive straight back as you enter, but after lifting *uke*'s leg turn somewhat to your left.

UCHI MATA SUKASHI
(inner-thigh throw reversal)

This is a popular counter to a fast *uchi mata* (page 96). To perform it you must sense the oncoming attack, slide your leg out of the way so that *uke* misses it, then use your hands to throw *uke* forward in a rolling motion.

Key points:

- Bring your left knee close to your right knee as quickly as possible so *uke*'s attacking leg cannot catch it.
- Pull with your left hand and push with your right as you throw *uke* forward.
- Bring your body close to increase power.

Leg throws (ashi waza)

Ashi waza are throws that rely primarily on attacking an opponent's lower body with your legs or feet. In some you move *uke*'s feet out from under him; in others you stop his feet from moving when his upper body continues in motion. *Ashi waza* tend to be fast attacks that rely on catching your opponent at a weak moment, so accurate timing is the most critical element.

Because strength is less of a factor, *ashi waza* are often effective against larger opponents. Many are used in combination with other throws. Skill in *ashi waza* helps make other throws possible and allows you to attack from a greater distance than other types of techniques. They are equally important for breaking down a strong defense and against someone trying to advance on you.

In leg throws you generally reap, sweep, hook, or block your opponent's leg or legs. Reaping (*gari*) throws involve cutting out *uke*'s leg as if you are swinging a scythe; sweeping (*harai*) throws involve more subtle timing so *uke*'s foot is moved as his weight shifts towards it. Hooking (*gake*) throws trap *uke*'s weight-bearing foot in place as you push *uke* over it. Blocking (*sasae*) and wheeling (*guruma*) throws use your leg to stop *uke* from advancing or retreating while your hands drive *uke* over.

DEASHI HARAI
(forward or advancing foot sweep)

This is one of the simplest throws to learn, but applying it in practice is quite difficult. Because timing is crucial, practice it repeatedly in *randori*. Used against an untrained opponent it can be both easy and devastating.

Uke will be stepping forward, shifting weight from the back foot to the front foot. To do so, *uke* must lean slightly forward and have some forward momentum. Once the forward motion starts, *uke* is committed to stepping and cannot go back without putting the front foot on the ground. Your task is to continue *uke*'s forward motion while sweeping *uke*'s foot out before too much weight is placed on it. Avoid sweeping too early before *uke* has committed to the step, or too late after weight is placed on the foot and it cannot be moved. Do not give away your intentions by any strong hand action until after you have swept the foot. Invite *uke* to come willingly towards you.

Key points:

- Try to sweep with the sole of your foot, placing the ball of your foot around *uke*'s heel, and keep your sweeping leg almost straight so you feel the power of your hips in the sweep.
- Sweep *uke*'s foot forward in the direction it is moving, or somewhat across *uke*'s body.
- Pull your left hand down following your left leg, and push your right hand toward your left. Use your hands as if you are turning the steering wheel on a large truck.

Deashi harai is a popular throw to set up an opponent for *tai otoshi* (page 74) or *harai goshi* (page 64). It can be applied from quite a distance, and with only a one-handed grip on *uke*'s sleeve. To escape the throw *uke* must either put weight on the front foot so it cannot be swept, or put weight on the back foot and lift the front foot out of the sweep. *Uke* can then counterattack with *tsubame gaeshi* (page 100).

HIZA GURUMA (knee wheel)

This was a favourite throw of Dutchman Anton Geesink, who was awarded the rank of 10th dan by the IJF, and was the first non-Japanese judo competitor to win the World Championships (1961) and Olympic gold (1964).

It takes advantage of *uke*'s forward motion to throw. As *uke* advances, add your own power to help *uke* advance even faster, then stop *uke* from stepping forward while continuing the momentum of the upper body in a circular motion.

Key points:

- Step quickly to the right and turn towards your left while pulling *uke* around you with your left hand.
- Place the sole of your left foot on the bottom side of *uke*'s right kneecap to prevent *uke* from stepping.
- Keep your left leg almost straight and continue your turn to the left to throw uke over your left leg.

This throw is often combined with *osoto gari* (page 90) and countered by grabbing the attacking leg and trying *kuchiki taoshi* (page 85) or *ouchi gari* (page 92).

SASAE TSURIKOMI ASHI
(propping lifting pulling throw)

This throw is embodied in the *samurai* saying, "When the enemy comes welcome him; when he goes send him on his way." First invite *uke* in close, then block the advancing ankle with speed and accuracy as you move out of the way so *uke* flies past. Fearlessly draw *uke* into you and then twist with sudden determination to bring *uke* around you and to the ground.

Key points:

- Bring the sole of your left foot strongly against the front of *uke*'s advancing right ankle.
- Keep *uke* close to you, bringing your own right hip near *uke*'s left hip.
- Rotate your body strongly to your left bringing *uke* around with you.

OSOTO GARI (large outer reap)

This powerful throw, frequently used in self-defense and tournaments, is a favorite of Yasuhiro Yamashita, who won four World Championships leading up to his Olympic gold medal in 1984.

To perform this throw, push with your hands and body to *uke*'s right rear corner, then continue relentlessly to drive into *uke* as you sweep out the supporting leg, causing *uke* to fall backwards. Keep your toes pointed and your leg strong, making your body one long lever as you reap.

Key points:

- As you drive forward, pull *uke* around you and across your chest with your left hand.
- Bring your right leg and hip through very far for a powerful sweep.
- As you sweep, bring your head down and your foot up at least as high as your head, and at the same time twist to your left.

Osoto gari can be combined with *harai goshi* (page 64) or *hiza guruma* (page 89). The basic counter is *osoto gaeshi* (opposite). *Harai goshi* (page 64) may also be used.

OSOTO GAESHI (large outer reap counter)

In this counter your opponent is attacking you with *osoto gari* (opposite). Respond by blocking the attack, stepping back onto your left foot to regain your balance, then throw with an *osoto gari* of your own.

Key points:
- When you step back with your left foot, turn it to the left.
- Pull *uke*'s left arm to your left, and push *uke*'s head to your left as you turn to your left.
- Once *uke* is off balance, reap out the leg.

OSOTO OTOSHI (large outer drop)

This is similar to *osoto gari* (opposite), but in the final throwing action you do not reap *uke*'s leg out; you cut *uke* down by slicing your leg into the back of *uke*'s leg to bend his knee, break his posture, and make him drop to the mat.

Key points:
- Raise your attacking leg high, with a bent knee.
- Try to place your foot at the top of *uke*'s thigh, then drive it down between *uke*'s legs as you straighten it.
- Push *uke* straight down onto his back.

OSOTO GURUMA (large outer wheel)

This is similar to *osoto gari* (page 90), but both *uke*'s legs are blocked while *uke* is thrown directly backward. *Uke*'s legs must be relatively close together for it to work. Use it as a counter or follow-up to *osoto gari* and *kosoto gari* (page 96). To defeat it, use *osoto gaeshi* (page 91).

Key points:
- Both hands force *uke* down to the rear.
- Step in very deep and keep your body close to *uke*. Your right hip must penetrate past *uke*'s hip.
- Place your right leg across *uke*'s legs, your right ankle behind *uke*'s left knee. Drive back and down.

OUCHI GARI (large inner reap)

This technique is often used by the 1987 World Champion, Mike Swain, of the United States. Perform the basic throw while *uke* is advancing with the left leg, reaping it out as it moves forward, causing *uke* to fall. There are many possible variations, set-ups, and follow-ups.

Key points:
- As *uke* steps forward, pull *uke* more forward with your right hand so the right side of your chest comes in contact with *uke*'s chest.
- Place your right leg behind *uke*'s and reap it in the direction it is moving.
- *Uke* should fall backward toward the leg being reaped. This technique is often used in combination with *uchi mata* (page 96) or *kouchi gari* (page 95) because your leg is already between *uke*'s. To counter it use *ouchi gaeshi* (opposite) or *tani otoshi* (page 105).

OUCHI GAESHI (large inner reap counter)

When you are attacked with *ouchi gari* against your left leg, sweep *uke's* leg across your body and throw *uke* to your left. A variation of this throw is to rotate *uke* to the right as you escape the reap, throwing with a motion such as *uki otoshi* (page 79).

Key points:

- Control *uke's* head as the attack begins.
- Rotate your upper body to the left, bringing *uke* with you.
- Use your entire leg to sweep *uke's* leg to your right.

Variation

KOSOTO GAKE (small outer hook)

This is similar to *kosoto gari* (page 96) except that you do not reap *uke*'s foot out. Instead, you hold it in place so it cannot move and you push *uke* over it.

Key points:

- Hook your heel around the back of *uke*'s heel.
- Pull down and to your left with your left hand, while pushing *uke* back and to your left with your right hand.
- Try to pin all of *uke*'s weight onto the outside edge of *uke*'s right heel.

This throw may also be done in a very low version where you wrap your leg around *uke*'s ankle so that your knee is behind *uke*'s heel. You may be able to follow this throw with *osoto gari* (page 90) if *uke* escapes. *Uchi mata* (page 96) is the most common counter throw.

KOUCHI GARI (small inner reap)

This is an especially effective throw against an opponent whose legs are spread too far apart. Whenever your opponent's feet are more than shoulder width apart, you should be able to reap one foot out with this throw.

Key points:

- Use this throw when *uke* is stepping forward.
- Use the sole of your right foot behind *uke*'s right heel to reap it from the inside in the direction of *uke*'s toes.
- Pull *uke* to your left with your left hand while your body and right arm push *uke* backward.

Kouchi makikomi is another version: grab the leg you are attacking with your right arm, as well as your right foot; place your right shoulder into *uke*'s right hip, push to *uke*'s right rear corner, and roll down on top of *uke*.

Kouchi gari is often combined with *ouchi gari* (page 92) or *uchi mata* (page 96) into an integrated attack. It can be countered with a well-timed *hiza guruma* (page 89) or *tani otoshi* (page 105).

Variation: *kouchi makikomi*

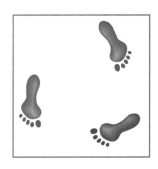

KOSOTO GARI (small outer reap)

This small reap is applied to *uke*'s foot, rather than the entire leg as in *osoto gari*, which is a big reaping action. As there is less power in a smaller reaping movement you need better timing and less weight on the foot you are attacking. This throw is usually used while *uke* is moving forward onto the foot you want to attack.

Key points:

- Use this throw when *uke* is stepping forward.
- Use the sole of your foot behind *uke*'s heel to reap it forward in the direction that uke's toes are pointing.
- Pull *uke* to your left with your left hand while your body and right arm push *uke* backward.

  Nidan kosoto gari is a variation usually applied when the foot you would normally attack with *kosoto gari* is in the air, so you reap out the other foot. It is sometimes combined with *kosoto gari*. As you attack, *uke* may lift his right foot to escape; quickly apply *nidan kosoto gari* by reaping the left foot out while you continue pushing *uke* backwards. You can counter a weak *kosoto gari* attack with *osoto gari* (page 90), or a more powerful attack by turning into *uchi mata* (below).

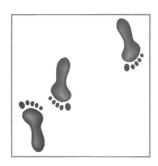

UCHI MATA (inner-thigh throw)

This is one of the most powerful and popular throws in competitive judo. Although classified as a leg throw in the *Nage no Kata*, it can also be applied with a significant amount of hip action.

Key points:

- Pull *uke* forward to create the *kuzushi*, or apply the technique when *uke* is off balance to the front.
- With your upper thigh, attack anywhere between *uke*'s left thigh and right thigh.
- As your leg sweeps up, put your head down, bringing *uke* with you.

  Use *uchi mata* after trying attacks with *ouchi gari* (page 92) or *kouchi gari* (page 95). The primary counter is *uchi mata sukashi* (page 85).

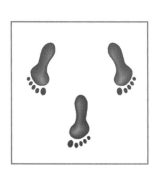

ASHI GURUMA (leg wheel)

Pull *uke* forward, then quickly block the advancing leg and pull *uke* over it. This throw is similar in principle to *hiza guruma* (page 89), but with the difference that you are facing the opposite direction and applying the technique with the opposite foot.

Key points:

- Place your right leg across *uke*'s right leg around the knee.
- Continue a strong pull around you and down with your left hand while pushing with your right.
- Throw *uke* straight forward, although you can also throw more towards the side.

HARAI TSURIKOMI ASHI
(lifting pulling foot sweep)

This looks somewhat like *sasae tsurikomi ashi* (page 89). However, it is applied when *uke* is retreating rather than advancing, and *uke*'s legs are swept out rather than simply blocked.

Key points:

- As *uke*'s left foot steps back, enter close and place the sole of your right foot on the front of *uke*'s left ankle.
- Keeping your right leg straight, sweep *uke*'s left foot back and to your left.
- Simultaneously pull *uke*'s upper body around you to your right.

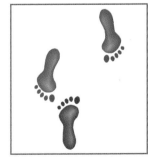

O GURUMA (large wheel)

This is a forward throw similar in appearance to *harai goshi* (page 64). The difference is that your leg contacts *uke* higher and you are further away from *uke* so your leg cannot sweep and only blocks while you wheel *uke*'s chest over it. This was a specialty of Kyuzo Mifune, one of only 12 10th degree black belts ever promoted by the Kodokan. He found it an easy way for a small person to throw a larger person.

Key points:
- As *uke* is coming forward, use the spinning entry shown below, and place your thigh just below *uke*'s waist.
- Continue bringing *uke*'s upper body forward with your hands and your turning motion.
- Use your leg like a bar to roll *uke* over.

OKURIASHI HARAI (following foot sweep)

As *uke* moves sideways or in a circular motion, the feet generally slide apart and then together. This throw takes advantage of this natural motion by sliding *uke*'s feet further to the side so they slip out from under *uke* as if they are on ice. Always sweep *uke*'s feet in the direction they are moving to accelerate their motion, while stopping *uke*'s upper body from following. Use this throw when *uke* is stepping around you or directly to the side. The faster *uke* is moving, the better the throw will work, but your timing must be impeccable.

Key points:

• Use the sole of your foot on the outside of *uke*'s ankle to sweep it sideways towards *uke*'s other foot.
• Keep your sweeping leg relatively straight in line with your torso so you use the power of your entire body as one long, co-ordinated lever.
• Lift and turn *uke*'s upper body with your hands.

When your foot's sweeping action misses, follow up with *tai otoshi* (page 74) or *harai goshi* (page 64). This throw can be countered with *tsubame gaeshi* (page 100), or you can step through and apply *tai otoshi* or *harai goshi*.

TSUBAME GAESHI (swallow counter)

When your opponent tries *deashi harai* (page 88) against you, lift your foot off the mat and quickly sweep the attacking foot with your own *deashi harai*. Your foot will make a quick circular motion like the flight of a swallow.

Key points:

- Try to move your foot out of the way just before *uke* makes contact with your foot.
- Bend your knee without moving your upper leg so your foot comes back quickly; then straighten your knee again to place your foot against *uke*'s foot.
- Take control of the throw with your hands.

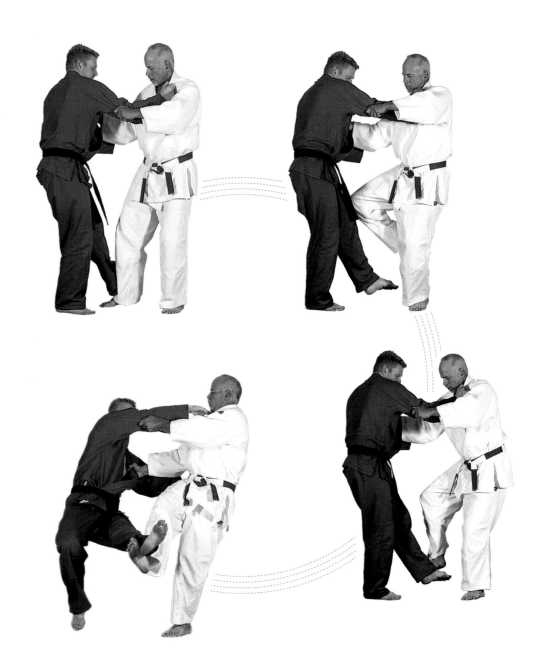

UCHI MATA GAESHI (inner thigh throw counter), *HARAI GOSHI GAESHI* (sweeping hip throw counter), *HANE GOSHI GAESHI* (spring hip throw counter)

These three techniques differ mainly in the attacks that are offered by *uke*. In each case you counter *uke*'s attempted throw—*uchi mata* (page 96), *harai goshi* (page 64), or *hane goshi* (page 65)—by throwing *uke* to the side or back corner. *Uchi mata gaeshi* is shown below.

Key points:

- Pull your right hand back and step to your left as *uke* enters for the throw, bringing *uke* off balance to the left.
- Place your left foot around *uke*'s supporting leg.
- Continue moving *uke* to the left, blocking or sweeping out *uke*'s supporting leg with your left foot or leg.

Sacrifice throws (sutemi waza)

Any technique in which you must give up your standing position and fall to the ground to throw your opponent is called a sacrifice throw. Sacrifice means you intentionally put yourself in danger in order to gain a greater objective.

Sacrifice throws are risky in free practice and tournaments; if your attempt is unsuccessful your opponent will usually be in a superior position over you. Even so, sacrifice techniques are often attempted in international competition, and can be extremely effective because they use gravity more than strength to build momentum. *Sutemi waza* skills allow you to get as low as possible under your opponent, while using your entire body weight to add power.

There are traditionally two types of sacrifice throws: those where you fall to your side (*yoko sutemi waza*); and those where you fall to your back (*ma sutemi waza*). The lines between these groups are often blurred because some throws can be done either way.

TOMOE NAGE (circular throw)

Use *tomoe nage* when *uke* is advancing strongly or leaning forward. It also works well against an opponent who is using stiff arms to prevent you from getting close. As *uke* pushes, you suddenly give way, like a dam breaking, so *uke* crashes forward and tumbles down. This throw is seen quite often in tournaments, and in movies.

Key points:
- Grip high on *uke*'s upper body for maximum leverage.
- Place your foot low on *uke*'s hip as you fall onto your back.
- Pull strongly with your hands throughout the throw so that *uke* comes forward and down.

Other variations of this throw include a two-foot version, and *yoko tomoe nage*, where you fall to your side under *uke* to throw. Foot sweeps often lead into *tomoe nage* attacks. A well-timed *ouchi gari* (page 92) or *kouchi gari* (page 95) will usually work as a counter.

Variation: *yoko tomoe nage*

SUMI GAESHI (corner reversal)

This is typically used against an opponent in a bent-over, defensive posture. It is similar to *tomoe nage* except the foot position is not as high on *uke*, which makes it easier to do against an opponent who is in a very low posture, or who is very close to you. *Sumi gaeshi* is very similar to sweeps used to roll over an opponent once you are on your back on the ground, so learning it will help in other grappling situations as well.

Key points:

• Pull *uke* forward and down, controlling *uke*'s right arm.
• As you fall to your back under *uke* place the top of your right foot on the inside of *uke*'s thigh.
• Use your foot to lift *uke* as your hands pull *uke* forward (*uke* rolls over his right shoulder).

TANI OTOSHI (valley drop)

Tani otoshi is often used as a counterattack to a hip or shoulder throw, but can also be applied when *uke* pulls back to recover from your attempted hip throw. *Uke* should feel as if his feet are on the edge of a cliff and he is falling backward into a deep valley.

Key points:

• Drive your right leg behind both of *uke*'s legs.
• Keep *uke*'s side tight against your chest.
• Turn towards *uke* as you fall to your right side.

UKI WAZA (floating technique)

Uki waza is performed lightly with little physical contact, so *uke* rolls like a tumbleweed blown through a desert town.

Key points:
- Slide your left leg in very far so your upper thigh blocks *uke's* advancing right foot.
- Use your falling weight to bring *uke* forward and down.
- Turn to your left side as you throw *uke* over your left shoulder.

YOKO OTOSHI (side drop)

This is similar to *uki waza* (above) except for the direction of the throw. As you drop to your side, throw *uke* directly sideways over your outstretched leg, not forward as in *uki waza*.

Key points:
- Slide your left leg in very far so your upper thigh comes close to the outside of *uke's* right foot.
- Use your falling weight to pull *uke* off balance to the side.
- Turn your body towards your left side as you throw.

YOKO WAKARE (side separation)

For this throw, roll *uke* over and around your upper body as you fall directly on your side in front of *uke*. Your falling action brings *uke* forward and down, while rotating your body rolls *uke* over you.

Key points:
- Fall directly in front of *uke* as *uke* is pushing forward and advancing.
- Pull *uke*'s upper body tightly to you as you fall so that *uke* is sure to come down with you.
- As you fall, twist strongly to your left bringing *uke* over you.

YOKO GURUMA (side wheel)

This is commonly used as a counter to an opponent's strong forward hip or shoulder throw. Go with the attacker's throwing action, even accelerating it, falling in front of *uke* and pulling *uke* over you to complete the throw. *Uke*'s own drive forward causes him to fall over you. This is seldom used in tournaments because in a good *yoko guruma* there is no break between your opponent's attack and your application of *yoko guruma*, so the referee often gives the score to your opponent when you fall onto your back, not considering that he was subsequently thrown.

Key points:
- As *uke* attempts a hip throw, slide around the attacking hip, swinging your right leg deep between *uke*'s legs.
- Place your left hand around *uke*'s waist and your right hand on *uke*'s stomach.
- Fall under *uke*, between *uke*'s legs, and roll *uke* over your left shoulder.

URA NAGE (back throw)

When *uke* attacks weakly for a hip or shoulder throw, drop low to pick *uke* up and throw him over your shoulder as you fall to your back. Commonly called a suplex in wrestling, this throw can be done easily without any grip on the *judogi*. *Uke* can stop or counter this throw by hooking a leg, as in *ouchi gari* (page 92).

Key points:
- As *uke* comes close for a hip or shoulder throw, bend your legs to get low under *uke*.
- Grab tightly around *uke*'s waist to hold *uke*'s body against your chest.
- Lift *uke* by straightening your legs and thrusting your hips forward, then fall to your back, throwing *uke* over your left shoulder.

HIKIKOMI GAESHI (pulling-in counter)

This throw is used against an opponent in a bent-over, defensive position. It can also be used when your opponent is on hands and knees in front of you. Pull *uke*'s head down so you can put your chest on it. With your left arm grab under *uke*'s right arm and place your hand on *uke*'s right shoulder blade. Grab the back of *uke*'s belt with your right hand.

Key points:
- Using your left hand for leverage, push *uke*'s right shoulder up. When *uke* resists, reverse direction and pull the shoulder down as you fall under *uke*.
- Rotate to your right as you slide under *uke*.
- Pull *uke*'s belt to bring *uke* over you.

YOKO GAKE (side hook)

In *yoko gake* you block *uke*'s feet from moving as you fall down on your side, with *uke* falling next to you like a tall tree after it is chopped off at the bottom. This technique is usually studied in depth when learning the *Nage no Kata*.

Key points:

- Using your hands, straighten *uke* upright as you pull *uke*'s right sleeve into your chest, bringing his weight onto his right foot.
- Place your left foot against the side of *uke*'s advanced right foot, continuing until *uke* lands.
- Fall to your left side, bringing *uke* down next to you.

TAWARA GAESHI (rice bale counter)

This is typically used as a counter to *morote gari* (page 82) or any double-leg takedown or forward tackle. It can also be performed against an opponent in a bent-over, defensive posture.

Key points:

- As *uke* grabs around your waist or legs, lean over *uke*'s back and reach around *uke*'s waist from behind with both hands.
- Clasp your hands together in front of *uke*'s stomach.
- Sit back, bringing *uke*'s head down, lift up with your hands, and roll *uke* forward over your shoulder as you roll onto your back.

DAKI WAKARE (high lift and separate)

This is normally used when *uke* has hands and feet on the ground after falling forward attempting a throw. It may not result in a high score, but you will be able to continue on the ground from a good position.

Key points:

- Grab around *uke*'s waist from behind.
- Roll over *uke* to the right side.
- Hold tightly as you roll so you bring *uke* with you; *uke* rolls over you, landing to your left.

KANI BASAMI (crab scissors)

Officially banned in tournaments after the Japanese champion, Yasuhiro Yamashita, was injured by this technique in a tournament leading up to the 1984 Olympic Games, this is nevertheless a strong, deceptive throw that is useful for self-defense.

Key points:

- Pull your opponent upright and backwards, particularly with your right hand.
- Put your right leg in front of *uke*'s abdomen as your left leg goes behind *uke*'s knees (or lower).
- Scissor your legs and turn to the right, sweeping *uke*'s legs out and pulling *uke* backward.

KAWAZU GAKE (one-leg entanglement)

Kawazu gake is not permitted in judo competition because of possible knee injuries. It involves wrapping your leg around your opponent's, sometimes called grape vining, and then falling backward on top of, or next to, *uke*. *Uke*'s leg is straightened and if you fall on it the knee may be hyper-extended.

Key points:

- Slide your right leg between *uke*'s legs and wrap your foot around to the front of *uke*'s shin.
- Lift this trapped leg in front of you.
- Fall to your side or back, bringing *uke* down with you.

OSOTO MAKIKOMI (large outer wraparound)

This and the following *makikomi* throws (*see* pages 112–113) rely on the principle of rotating your body while holding *uke*'s right arm tightly to you so that *uke*'s body is wrapped around yours like a cord around a spool. As you continue to wrap and fall, *uke* rolls over you and is brought down underneath you.

Osoto makikomi is used as a counter or follow-up to an *osoto gari* (page 90) attack.

Key points:

- Attempt *osoto gari* (page 90) and pull *uke* strongly with your left hand.
- *Uke*'s right arm must be wrapped well around your upper body so that *uke*'s shoulder is tight against your shoulder.
- Your twisting and rolling must be relentless; use your entire body weight to bring *uke* off balance and onto his back.

SOTO MAKIKOMI (outer wraparound throw)

This throw relies on strong rotation over your back, so your hips must enter deeply.

Key points:

• Do not let your upper body separate from *uke*.

• Keep *uke*'s shoulder under your armpit as you roll forward.

UCHI MAKIKOMI (inner wraparound throw)

This is similar to *soto makikomi* (above) except that your right arm is under *uke*'s right arm rather than over it. The rolling throwing action is the same.

Key points:

• Enter your hips more deeply in front of *uke* than you would for *seoi nage* (page 70).

• Once *uke* is locked to your back, roll toward your right shoulder, bringing *uke* with you.

UCHI MATA MAKIKOMI
(inner thigh wraparound)

After attempting an *uchi mata* (page 96), continue your forward pull directly into *uchi mata makikomi* by rolling forward and bringing yourself onto the ground, but with your opponent under you.

Key points:
* The hand position is normally the same as in *soto makikomi* (opposite), but sometimes *uke*'s head is included in the grip.
* You will land directly on top of *uke*.

HARAI MAKIKOMI (sweeping wraparound)

After entering for *harai goshi* (page 64), continue your forward pull directly into *harai makikomi* by twisting to the left and rolling forward, bringing *uke* with you.

Key points:
* Continue to pull powerfully with your left hand until you land on *uke*.
* Maintain tight body contact throughout the throw.

HANE MAKIKOMI
(springing wraparound throw)

After attacking with *hane goshi*, continue your forward pull directly into *hane makikomi* by twisting to your left, maintaining good contact and rolling forward.

Key points:
* Your right hand may slip off *uke*'s head to increase your rotation.
* *Uke* should land directly under you as you roll forward.

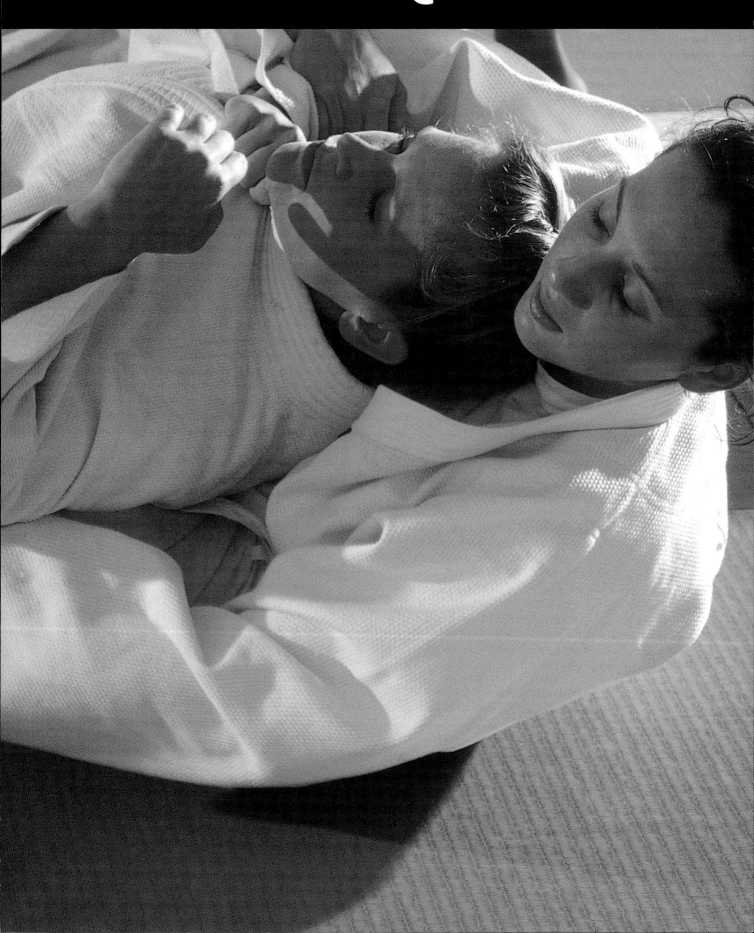

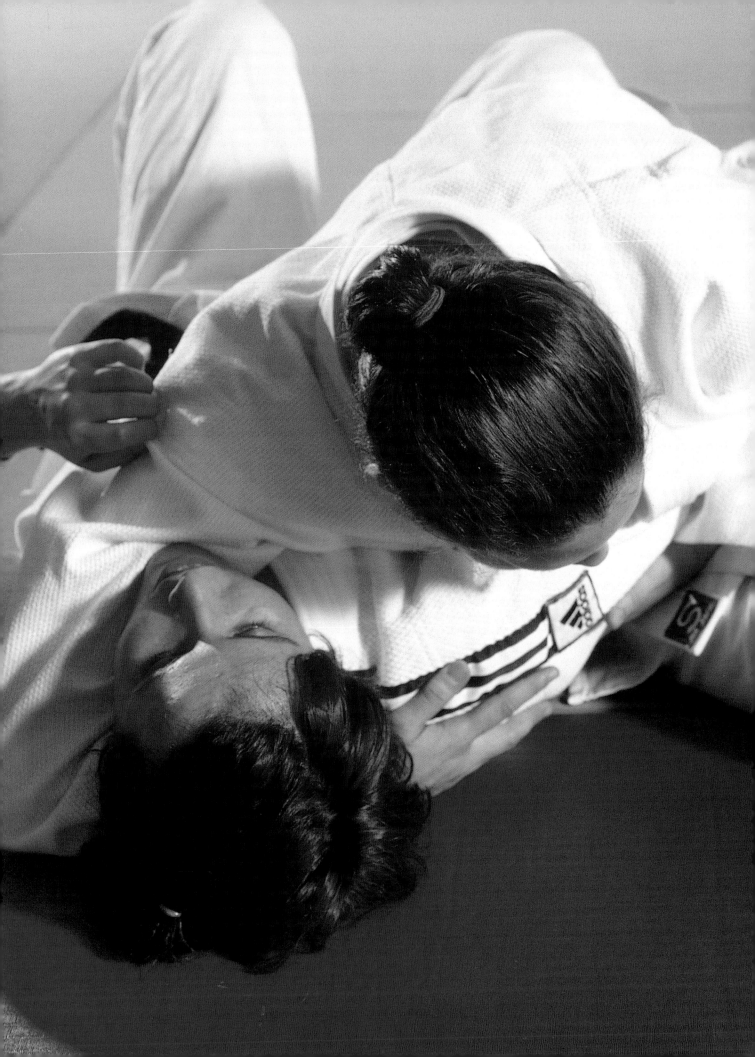

Pinning (osaekomi waza)

Judo grappling techniques consist of pins, chokes, strangulations, arm locks, and other joint locks. Many grappling techniques, particularly arm locks, can be performed either standing or on the ground, but pins are always used to immobilize an opponent on the mat. All grappling on the ground is called matwork, or *ne waza*.

Whether you are training for competition or self-defense, you must master transitions from standing techniques to ground techniques, and the basic positions of judo *ne waza*.

The focus of *osaekomi waza* is to learn the basics of control and how to maintain a superior position on the ground. Knowing the final hold is only a small part of the skill needed to get an opponent into a vulnerable position, so other grappling situations must be studied as well. The pins and positions in this chapter are a small sample.

As you practice techniques on the ground, try to maintain a sense of fluidity by staying relaxed and using your strength to fullest advantage through leverage and balance. Yield to superior power and redirect it to your advantage. Maintain a stable base by keeping your center of gravity low. Strive to control at least one part of your opponent, then work to expand your control. Flexibility in applying technique is the key.

Basic grappling control: the pin

Pinning skills are an important part of judo grappling because they teach you how to control an opponent, and conversely how to prevent or escape another person's control. These are essential lessons before moving on to strangulations or joint locks, where lack of control can lead to failure or injury. Pins are considered the basic control positions of judo grappling on the ground, and mastering the basics is always the key to success in more advanced studies.

In an ideal pin, you should be able to safely hold an opponent as long as necessary without hurting him or her. This gives you many self-defense options, including an opportunity to de-escalate a dangerous situation. You may also be able to make an opponent submit from pressure, pain, exhaustion, or suffocation. Finally, you can keep your opponent in a vulnerable position so you can apply more dangerous techniques, such as strikes or joint locks, if necessary.

Using pinning techniques you can easily control someone from a superior position. This conserves your energy and gives you various options to use a greater amount of force if needed. While holding a pin, you are generally free to get up and escape at any time. Pins are among the gentlest skills in judo, yet they are very effective for protecting yourself, and for subduing an adversary when necessary.

JUDO IS LIKE WATER

The nature of judo is often compared with that of water.

- Like judo *ne waza*, water is the humblest of all the elements as it always seeks the low point, but in the end it always overcomes.
- Water is soft and follows the path of least resistance, yet is vital for life.
- It can be as serene as a lily pond or as wild as the stormy sea.
- It can split rocks when it freezes or wear them away one drop at a time.
- Water is most serviceable to life when in its liquid state; judo is most effective when your technique is applied in a fluid manner.
- Remember that when water and fire wage war, water will be the victor.
- Water covers most of the earth yet its vast depths are largely unexplored.

What is a pin?

A pin in judo is a control hold that keeps your opponents on their backs and prevents them from rising. For a pin to count in competition it must be applied from above (that is, you must be on top). You cannot be between your opponent's legs, and your position must be face down (as in *kami shiho gatame* – page 121) or on your side (as in *kesa gatame* – page 120). For the pin to be valid in tournaments, you cannot be upright or lying face-up on your back.

To score a winning point (*ippon*) you must maintain control and prevent escape for 25 seconds. Judo competition statistics show that practically no one can escape from a pin if they cannot do so within the first 25 seconds. A smaller point is awarded for a hold of shorter duration: 20 to 24 seconds is *waza ari*, 15 to 19 seconds is *yuko*, and 10 to 14 seconds is *koka*.

Each pinning technique has multiple variations. The term for a variation is *kuzure*, so *kuzure kesa gatame* is a modified version of the basic *kesa gatame*. While executing kesa gatame, you could move your hands to any other position and it would still be considered a variation of the basic *kesa gatame*. Only five basic ways of pinning are recognized by the Kodokan, but nine techniques are used sufficiently in international competition to be recognized by the International Judo Federation.

Principles

Balance is a key component of success in pinning, as it is in standing judo. The basic principles of *kuzushi* (or unblancing the opponent) that make throws work are also important on the ground. When you stand with two feet on the ground, you are easily moved and your balance is naturally more precarious; when you are on the ground it is much more difficult to lose your balance. This is one of the reasons Jigoro Kano emphasized standing techniques as a means for teaching the secrets of *kuzushi*. Once learned, your sense of balance and skills in off-balancing can help dramatically on the ground.

Several factors affect the stability of an object when outside forces are exerted on it, whether it is a building, a person standing, or a person pinning.

- Height: the lower or shorter an object, the better the balance.
- Center of gravity: the closer the center of gravity to the center point of the base, the better the balance.
- Base: the wider the base in each direction, the better the balance.
- Friction: the greater the friction between the body and the ground, the more difficult it is to unbalance.

- Mass: the heavier an object, the more difficult it is to unbalance.
- Rigidity: the more flexible and responsive to forces, the better the balance.

In every pin, try to keep a wide base (e.g. legs spread), stay as low as possible, keep as much weight as you can on your opponent, and move your body in a relaxed manner to respond to your opponent's actions. The opposite is true when trying to escape. To escape, try to restrict or take advantage of your opponent's movement, get your opponent's center of gravity off his or her base, get your opponent as high as possible off the ground, and make your opponent's base as small as possible.

When you are on the bottom, space is your friend; when you are on top, it is your enemy. To prevent a pin or escape from it, create as much space as possible between you and an opponent. Conversely, to pin someone, remove any space between you. When you are on top, get as close as possible to the opponent so you can effectively apply your weight and restrict the opponent's movement.

The best escapes start long before you are pinned; you must prevent your opponent from getting a better position than you. Once a pin is successfully locked on, the person on top has a clear advantage that can only be overcome with superior skill. An immediate defense or counterattack is needed before your opponent gains complete control.

Below: A strong pin establishes the control needed to apply arm locks or other submissions.

KESA GATAME (scarf hold)

This is called the scarf hold because you wrap yourself around *uke*'s head and body like a sash. You should be able to hold someone without much effort when you have the right position. Distinct variations include *kuzure kesa gatame* (modified scarf hold), *makura kesa gatame* (pillow scarf hold), and *ushiro kesa gatame* (reverse scarf hold).

Kesa gatame can also be applied to make it difficult for your opponent to breathe. Encircle uke's right arm around your torso as you lean forward and grab high on the arm. Hold it tightly and rotate your body so *uke*'s right arm is pulled up and your body is pushed heavily onto *uke*'s chest to compress the lungs.

Key points:

- Keep control of *uke*'s arm and wrap it tightly around your body.
- Keep your legs spread for a solid base.
- Keep your head down, and control *uke*'s head by keeping it off the mat.

Variation: *kuzure kesa gatame* (1)

Variation: *ushiro kesa gatame*

Variation: *kuzure kesa gatame* (2)

Variation: *makura kesa gatame*

KATA GATAME (shoulder hold)

This can be applied as both a pin and a strangulation that forces your opponent to submit. To apply the strangulation, drive your weight down onto *uke*'s arm, which is then pressed into *uke*'s own neck. Your own arm around *uke*'s neck squeezes to complete the strangulation on both sides of the neck.

Key points:
- Hold *uke*'s head tightly to prevent movement or escape.
- Keep your head against *uke*'s head so *uke*'s arm cannot slip out.
- Drive your shoulder into *uke*'s neck while squeezing with your arm.

Variation

KAMI SHIHO GATAME (top four-corner hold)

This is a strong pin because you are on top of *uke*'s chest from above his head, so his legs cannot be used effectively to escape. Several variations are all called *kuzure kami shiho gatame* (modified top four-corner hold).

Key points:
- Hang on tightly to *uke*'s belt with your hands.
- Keep your legs spread apart to form a strong base.
- Keep your hips low and maintain your weight on your opponent while keeping in line with *uke*.

Variation: *kuzure kamishiho gatame*

YOKO SHIHO GATAME (side four-corner hold)

In this side-control hold your chest pushes down on *uke*'s chest. Variations include *kuzure yoko shiho gatame* (modified side four-corner hold) and *mune gatame* (chest hold).

Key points:

- Reach around *uke*'s leg to grab the belt, jacket, or pants, while the other hand reaches around *uke*'s neck to grab the collar or shoulder.
- Keep your legs spread apart to form a strong base.
- Keep your hips low and make sure you maintain your weight on your opponent.

Variation: *mune gatame*

Variation: *kuzure yoko shiho gatame* (1)

Variation: *kuzure yoko shiho gatame* (2)

TATE SHIHO GATAME (straight four-corner hold)
Mount your opponent with one leg on each side as you sit on *uke*'s abdomen. Hand and foot positions can vary and all variations are called *kuzure tate shiho gatame* (modified straight four-corner hold). Since your body is higher than *uke*'s and your legs are not spread as far as in most pins, keeping your balance requires greater skill. This pin is important for self-defense as you can control *uke* with your legs, freeing your hands to strike if necessary.

Key points:
- Keep your knees spread as much as possible.
- Control *uke*'s hips with your legs.
- Keep your arms relaxed so you can post them on the mat to stop *uke*'s attempts to roll you off.

Basic foot position

Variation of foot position

Variation of arm position

Variation of foot position

Basic ground positions

When both opponents are on the ground, four important positions must be mastered. One person will be either on his back (face up) or stomach (face down), with the other on top in either position. From each position, whether you are on top or bottom, you must learn to take the initiative. Trying to maintain your position defensively will only yield the opportunity to your opponent.

TIPS FOR GROUND FIGHTING:
- Movement should be fluid and natural.
- Maintain a wide, low base for stability.
- Utilize your weight to your advantage.
- Keep your arms close to your body.
- Always face your opponent.
- Keep your head above your hips.
- Use your feet like extra hands.

YOU ARE FACE DOWN—BOTTOM POSITION

A general rule in all martial arts is never to turn your back on your opponent. When you are face down on the ground, you are vulnerable to attack. If you are unavoidably on the ground face down with your opponent over you, first try to protect yourself by getting on your hands and knees (or elbows and knees). This is primarily a defensive position used in competition to avoid a pinning technique, to gain mobility, or to help your efforts to stand up. This position should only be used as a transition between lying face down on the mat and standing up, reversing the positions, or while turning to face your opponent to initiate an attack. Offensive options for the person on the bottom are much more limited than for the one on top, so the longer you stay in this position the more likely you will be defeated.

YOUR OPPONENT IS FACE DOWN
—TOP POSITION

The hands and knees position in judo is sometimes called the turtle position, because a defensive contestant may pull his or her arms in and cover the neck to protect from arm locks and chokes. In tournaments you will only have a short opportunity to begin to break down the turtle position. Your attacks must thus be drilled repeatedly against resisting opponents so you can create immediate progress. There are many ways to attack the turtle position with turnovers that lead to pins, arm locks, and chokes. Another option is to gain control from the back so you can apply arm locks, chokes, or strangulations from the rear.

YOU ARE FACE UP—BOTTOM POSITION

The guard position is when you are lying on your back with your opponent kneeling or standing between your legs. This may result in a stalemate, with neither contestant able to establish enough control to apply a pin, arm lock or choke. The person on the bottom uses his legs to control the top person and prevent attacks, while attempting to turn him over to gain a superior position. The person who is between the legs must try to get out from the legs so as to attack freely.

Once in this position in a judo tournament, the referee will only permit a short time for either contestant to make progress towards greater control. Although this position is primarily defensive for the person on the bottom, against a less skilled opponent it can easily become offensive because you can successfully attack in many ways, for instance, by sweeping out your opponent's legs to get on top, or applying an arm lock from the bottom, such as *ude hishigi juji gatame* (page 142) or *ude garami* (page 141).

When you are on your back with an opponent beside you, use your legs to gain control of your opponent before he or she secures a pin or uses another technique.

To defend against an opponent approaching from the right, immediately bring your right knee and elbow together in a position often called the shrimp. As you bring your knee and elbow in to block your opponent's advance, slide your hips away to create more space. This should provide the opportunity to wrap your legs around at least part of your opponent—and in this way begin the process of gaining control.

One rule of self-defense when you are on your back is always to keep your legs between yourself and your opponent. If your attacker begins to get around your legs, you need to continually push him back down to your legs while moving your body away. Your legs are much stronger than your arms, and can be used to keep an opponent further away because they are also longer.

When you are on your back protecting yourself from an attack, your defensive objective should always be to keep as much space as possible between you and your opponent. When you have sufficient confidence to begin an attack, you will want to control the space between you and your opponent and at that point you can begin to close the distance.

YOUR OPPONENT IS FACE UP—TOP POSITION

The person on top (between the legs) can also use various methods to escape and gain complete control. In this case, gravity is on your side and you can apply your weight onto your opponent. The more you lean onto your opponent, however, the less solid your base is, so be careful to keep your center of gravity low to prevent yourself from being rolled over. In general, keep your head higher than your hips and as much over your hips as you can, with your legs spread for a wide base. For every attempt you make at escaping the legs, your opponent has defenses and attacks, so try to keep your balance at all times as you try to improve your position. Focus on getting better control before attempting submissions.

Strangulation & choking (*shime waza*)

Choking and strangulation are subtle techniques that require more attention to detail than most other judo skills because the targets are usually small, specific areas of the neck that are often well protected by your opponent. Accuracy, not brute strength, is the key.

In some chokes, the hands use the lapel as if it were a thin cord to encircle the throat; in others, they twist or rotate powerfully into the neck; in yet others, they pull or push to apply pressure directly to the carotid arteries or trachea (windpipe). You can apply even the basic chokes effectively in multiple ways, depending on the position, relative size, and movement of your opponent, as well as your training, strengths, and preferences.

Principles

There are two basic ways of choking or strangling an opponent, as well as some combinations of the two:

- stopping or restricting the flow of blood to the brain by compressing the carotid arteries on one or both sides of the neck;
- stopping or reducing the flow of air to the lungs by directly compressing the trachea, blocking the mouth to keep the victim from inhaling (suffocation), or compressing the chest and lungs to prevent the opponent from inhaling (often used during pinning techniques).

These are sometimes distinguished by different terms and may be referred to as choking, strangling, wringing, or neck locks. However, they are grouped together as a class of grappling techniques called *shime waza*. *Shime* means constriction and *waza* means technique. The term choking technically refers to a blockage of the windpipe or mouth that prevents breathing, whereas strangulation means compression of the arteries in the neck to prevent blood from reaching the brain. In addition, pressure points, such as the nerves in the carotid triangle, can be attacked to cause unconsciousness.

Many of the *shime waza* can be applied in either or both of the methods described on page 129. Practice both as they are useful for various situations, but strangulation is generally stressed in most judo classes around the world. Compression of the carotid arteries is the most important form of *shime waza* because it requires the least force and is most in keeping with the efficiency principle of judo—maximum effect with minimum effort.

It is also the quickest way to produce unconsciousness and the most universally effective against various types and sizes of opponents.

Medical tests have established that the amount of pressure needed to block the arteries in strangulation is six times less than that required to choke someone by collapsing the airway. Directly stopping the blood supply to the brain also results in loss of consciousness at least six times faster than indirectly reducing oxygen in the brain through restricting breathing or the flow of air to the lungs.

Carotid strangulations are also safer and involve less pain than other *shime waza* methods, making them easier to practice. It is also easier to acquire sufficient skill to be confident in using them. This makes them more effective, and more compatible with another basic principle of judo—mutual welfare and benefit. A skilfully executed technique enables you to produce unconsciousness or submission with little pain or forewarning to your opponent. This makes it a powerful weapon in judo's arsenal of techniques.

Even though chokes and strangulations are extremely effective against unskilled opponents, only a small percentage of international judo contests are won with the use of *shime waza*. This is primarily because of various effective defences. Just as studying throws improves your balance and makes you harder to throw, training in *shime waza* should increase your awareness of vulnerabilities to chokes and strangles, and improve your ability to withstand such attacks.

The most important defensive rule is to keep your chin down and your shoulders up, so the target—your neck—is inaccessible to your opponent. Your hands can also protect your neck. Be aware of your opponent's attempts to grip your *judogi* in a way that enables a *shime waza* technique. For example, do not let your opponent get a grip high on your collar, or once this grip is secured, keep control of the other hand so it cannot finish the strangulation.

One unique aspect of *shime waza* techniques is that they can be applied from behind your opponent. To prevent this, never give your opponent your back or let your opponent get control of you from behind. If this does happen, immediately protect your neck while attempting to escape.

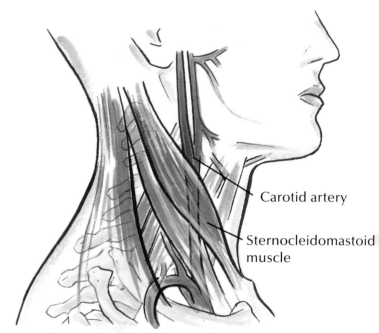

Carotid artery

Sternocleidomastoid muscle

Anatomy of a choke

Safety

Shime waza must be taught and supervised by a qualified instructor. Because the judo syllabus has always contained more well-developed strangulation and choking techniques than any other martial art, judo instructors usually have extensive experience with proper application. *Shime waza* are potentially dangerous and should be treated seriously. As taught in judo, though, they are temporary incapacitating techniques of short duration whose proper execution should be harmless. *Shime waza* have been used in judo classes and tournaments around the world for more than 120 years without a single reported fatality. Only with appropriate emphasis on safety and supervision can this record be maintained.

Care should be taken when teaching *shime waza* to children, whose physiology is less developed than that of adults. In most judo tournaments chokes are not permitted for children, so check the rules in your area. Children over the permissible age may learn basic *shime waza* with escapes and defenses, but always under strict supervision. Feeling different chokes or strangles being applied in practice, and learning when to submit, is an important form of preparation for tournament. For children—and beginners of any age—the emphasis should be on recognizing the effect of chokes or strangles, and protecting yourself while avoiding extreme pressure and unconsciousness in practice.

Shime waza may be practiced from either a standing position or on the ground, but the ground is inherently safer. When applying a standing *shime waza* with the intention of gaining the full effect, the victim will not be able to remain standing. In tournament and practice the person being strangled should always be taken to the ground immediately for better control and to prevent an accidental fall that could injure an opponent who becomes unconscious.

To avoid unnecessary periods of unconsciousness, learning when to give up is an important part of training. While you should not give up any opportunity to escape from *shime waza*, you must surrender once you recognize that defeat is inevitable and further resistance will cause unconsciousness. Once you allow yourself to be choked unconscious your life is literally in your opponent's hands, and the practice of any martial art requires you to learn ways of avoiding this ultimate helplessness. Because it is virtually impossible to speak while being choked, the universal signal for submission is repeatedly tapping the opponent or mat.

The most important safety rule for *shime waza* is to release pressure immediately after the opponent submits or begins to feel the effect of the technique. You should be sensitive enough—and have sufficient control—to recognize when *uke* begins to lose consciousness so that you can immediately release pressure even if *uke* does not tap. Loss of consciousness can be detected easily by sudden lack of resistance, the generally limp feeling of *uke*'s body, and a change in the colour of the face.

Top tips for effective strangulation

A good strangulation hold should render any opponent unconsciousness without injury or significant pain—in a matter of seconds. Here are the basic requirements.

- Ensure that your own body has complete freedom of action so you are in the best position for the technique you intend to use, and you are flexible enough to respond to *uke*'s attempts to escape. Your position should be stable so you can use the power of your entire body, not just your hands.
- Lead *uke* into a position in which it is most difficult to put up resistance, and control all *uke*'s actions. *Uke* must be unstable, off balance, and under your control as much as possible. Often this means stretching or straightening out *uke*'s body.
- Train your hands to get an accurate hold the moment you begin a technique, and make it work quickly. Once you begin the pressure, do not continually release to adjust your position. Firmly resolve not to let your opponent get away, but to continue until the end without slackening. Constant pressure is called for rather than extreme force. Excessive reliance on strength suggests defective technique because very little pressure is needed to compress an artery and render someone unconscious.

NAMI JUJI JIME (normal cross lock)

The first three strangulations are all called cross locks (*juji* means cross) because of the crossed position of your arms as you wring *uke*'s neck. They are similar in principle and appearance, though the exact position of the hands varies. The changes in hand position influence the ways each technique can be used.

For *nami juji jime*, cross your arms and grab *uke*'s collar high on each side of the neck. Place your thumbs inside the *judogi* so your palms face down. To apply strangulation, spread your elbows apart and up, wrapping your hands around *uke*'s neck. By hanging on tightly to the collar, the sides of your hands will roll the protective muscle forward and press on the carotid artery located on each side of *uke*'s neck. The pressure on the trachea should be minimal.

Key points:
- From the front, grab high on the collar, with thumbs in and arms crossed.
- Spread your elbows and expand your chest as you pull on the collar.
- Bring your head and chest close to your opponent.

Application from the rear

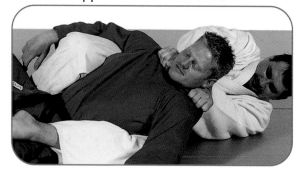

GYAKU JUJI JIME (reverse cross lock)

This is similar to *nami juji jime* (left) except your hands are reversed so that your palms are up and your fingers are inside uke's collar. This strangle is also applied by spreading your elbows and drawing your hands around the neck, though a different part of your hands will now compress the target arteries. To increase the effectiveness of this strangle, or to use the technique when *uke* is defending well and you cannot draw *uke* close, rotate your hands. As you hold the collar and try to turn your hands so that the palms face down, the side of your hand will be pressed into *uke*'s neck.

Key points:
- From the front, grab high on the collar, with your thumbs out and arms crossed.
- Spread your elbows and expand your chest as you pull on the collar.
- Bring your head and chest close to your opponent.

Application from the bottom

KATA JUJI JIME (half cross lock)

This is also similar to *nami juji jime* except that one hand grabs high on *uke*'s collar with the thumb in, while your other arm crosses under the first and you grab lower on the opposite collar or lapel with your fingers inside the *judogi*. The choking action comes primarily from your top hand on the collar wrapping around *uke*'s neck, while the other hand anchors the lapel down. The side of your choking hand applies pressure as in *nami juji jime*.

Key points:

- From the front, grab high on the collar, with your thumb in the judogi.
- With your other hand, grab the opposite lapel, with your fingers in; pull down.
- Bring your head and chest close to *uke* as you bring the hand on the collar around *uke*'s neck in a circular manner.

Defenses for all three of these cross locks:

In all the cross locks it is essential to bring *uke*'s neck close to your chest so your arms will have the maximum effect. The further away *uke* is, the less effective the strangulation. If you are attacked in this way, the simplest defense is to put both hands on your opponent's chest and push him away, preventing him from drawing you close or wrapping arms around your neck.

Another defense is to place the palm of your hand on your own cheek or neck before your opponent gets a grip with both hands, so that your hand protects your neck and is in the way of the strangulation. A third defense from a cross choke is to grab your opponent's elbows and push the one on top up, while pushing the one underneath down. This will effectively uncross his arms and allow your head to escape.

Application from standing

HADAKA JIME (naked lock)

This is called the naked lock because you do not use the *judogi* to apply the choking action as in other *shime waza*. Place your arm across the throat from behind your opponent to apply pressure directly to the trachea. This prevents breathing, and is very painful; usually your opponent will give up from the pain long before the choke takes effect. There are several variations of the basic choke, including versions that compress the arteries like other strangulations (sleeper holds).

Key points:

- Put *uke* into an off-balance position where you can control *uke*'s movement.
- Place the inside edge of your forearm or wrist against *uke*'s throat so that your palm is down.
- Place your shoulder behind *uke*'s head, and your head against the side of *uke*'s head, to control it.

Variation

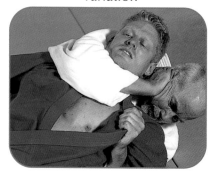

Variation

KATAHA JIME (single wing lock)

This is applied from the rear like *okuri eri jime* (page 135) except your left hand does not grab *uke*'s lapel. While your right hand strangles or chokes *uke*, your left hand controls *uke*'s head and left arm, making it difficult for *uke* to relieve the pressure on the neck or turn out of the *shime waza*.

Key points:

- Grab *uke*'s left lapel with your right hand across *uke*'s throat, controlling *uke*'s left arm with your left forearm.
- Slide your left hand to a position directly behind *uke*'s head or neck, usually with the back of your left hand against the base of *uke*'s head.
- *Uke*'s left arm should be pointing up over *uke*'s head as you apply the strangulation or choke.

Variation

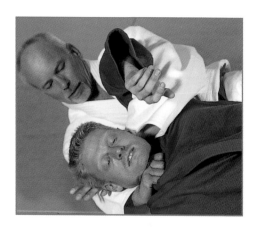

OKURI ERI JIME (sliding collar lock)

Another strangle from the rear, this uses the lapel like a cord wrapped around *uke*'s neck. In addition to the constricting action of the lapel, the inside edge of your right wrist or forearm compresses the carotid artery on one side of the neck. It can also be used as a choke, with the inside edge of your right forearm or wrist applying pressure directly on the trachea.

Key points:
- Put *uke* in an off-balance position completely under your control so *uke* cannot turn or curl up.
- Use your left hand to reach under *uke*'s left arm to grab *uke*'s right lapel, and pull it down towards *uke*'s waist.
- Pull *uke*'s left lapel around *uke*'s neck with your right hand.

A variation used as a counter to *seoi nage* (page 70)

KATATE JIME (one-hand choke)

This is similar to *kata juji jime* (page 133) except only one hand applies the choke without the assistance of the other hand. It can be performed from a variety of pins or positions in front of *uke*.

Key points:
- Immobilize *uke* completely.
- Grab *uke*'s lapel with one hand, with your thumb inside the *judogi*.
- Bring your elbow around *uke*'s throat, applying pressure directly on the trachea with your forearm.

RYOTE JIME (two-hand choke)

Here you apply pressure with your knuckles directly onto the area of the carotid arteries to stop the flow of blood to the brain.

Key points:
- Grab *uke*'s collar with both hands, one on each side.
- Get your thumbs inside the collar, approximately under *uke*'s ears.
- Pull with both hands and rotate your knuckles into each side of *uke*'s neck as you turn your palms upward.

Variation

SODE GURUMA JIME (sleeve wheel choke)

This is applied by gripping your own *judogi* to apply leverage into *uke*'s throat. It is most successful when you have control of *uke* between your legs from either the top or the bottom.

Key points:
- Place your left forearm behind *uke*'s head and grab *uke*'s collar or shoulder, or your own sleeve.
- Grab your own left sleeve with your right hand.
- Bring the outside edge of your right forearm down across *uke*'s throat in a circular motion.

TSUKKOMI JIME (thrust choke)

This works by thrusting your knuckles directly into the side of your opponent's neck. It may be applied as either a choke or strangulation, depending on the placement of your knuckles and how you use your opponent's lapel.

Key points:
- Grab *uke*'s left lapel with your right hand (thumb inside the *judogi*).
- Grip *uke*'s right lapel with your left hand (fingers inside the *judogi*, palm facing down).
- Pull with your right hand as you push your left hand directly into the side of *uke*'s neck, pulling the lapel across *uke*'s throat.

SANKAKU JIME (triangle choke)

This is a powerful choke that multiplies the strength of your legs and hips through leverage. It is difficult to escape and can be performed from the front, side, or back, and from above or below your opponent.

Key points:
- Trap *uke*'s head and one arm between your legs.
- Place your right foot behind your left knee.
- Bend your left leg as you pinch your knees together.

Joint locks (*kansetsu waza*)

Joint locks involve manipulating an opponent's joints by twisting, stretching, separating, or bending in any direction beyond their normal range. The aim is to compel an adversary to surrender because of pain from the beginning of a sprain or dislocation of the joint, particularly the elbow. If applied quickly and forcefully, joint locks can result in a sprain or dislocation or, in extreme circumstances, a broken bone.

Attacks against all joints were permitted in early judo contests, but for safety reasons joint locks have gradually been restricted in tournaments to the elbow only. In 1899, locks of the fingers, toes, wrists, and ankles were banned (knee entanglement or twisting knee locks were banned in 1916). Joint lock attacks were limited in contests to the elbow only in 1925 because of the severity of injuries resulting from attacking other joints with full force in contests.

Elbow joint locks have proved relatively safe because an opponent has ample opportunity to tap before injury can occur. They can be practiced in *randori* and tournaments without serious risk. Learning locks on the elbow helps in understanding all joint locks, but further study of joint locks against the knee, ankle, wrist, fingers, and spine is preserved in judo *kata*.

Principles

Modern arm locks aim to apply pressure to the elbow in one of two basic ways:

- The bent arm lock, *ude garami*.
- The straight arm lock (or arm bar), *ude hishigi ude gatame*.

In both cases, the key requirement is to control *uke's* body so *uke* cannot escape by moving. You must specifically control the shoulder, elbow and wrist of the arm being attacked. To apply leverage against the elbow, you normally immobilize the shoulder and then apply pressure against the wrist and the elbow in opposite directions to force submission or, if necessary, to dislocate the arm.

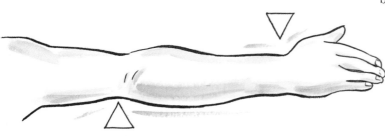

Leverage in straight arm bars creates more force than the joint can withstand.

Some arm locks can create tremendous force on the joint by utilizing all of your body, especially the hips, to apply pressure to the elbow. However, exact placement of the pressure on the fulcrum of the lever (the elbow) is essential for maximum efficiency, particularly against a stronger opponent. The fulcrum should generally be placed at the hollow just above the point of the elbow. You can feel this spot if you straighten your arm, place your finger on the point of the bone, then slide it towards your shoulder a few centimetres.

The exact position of the wrist is also important for skillful application of arm locks. In straight arm locks, pressure on the wrist should ideally be applied towards the little finger, away from the thumb. This makes it much more difficult for your opponent to turn out and escape from the arm bar.

Safety

Joint locks must be taught and supervised by a qualified instructor as they are potentially dangerous. Once you gain sufficient control over your opponent, you should be able to apply the technique with precision, providing opportunity for your opponent to signal defeat by tapping. In most practice and tournaments, arm locks are not permitted for children due to the fact that their bones are not yet fully developed. They are more susceptible to serious injury when practicing because they lack experience and maturity. For children and beginners of all ages, the emphasis should be on safety to guarantee years of healthy judo practice.

Arm locks may be practiced from either a standing position or on the ground, but the ground is usually safer. The victim of your arm lock can move around more freely when standing than on the ground. Because you have less control over an opponent's movement when he is standing, you may have to apply the technique more quickly for success and there is a greater likelihood of injury. In practice, take your opponent to the ground for better control and to prevent an accident.

The universal signal for submission is tapping the opponent or mat repeatedly. Learning when to tap is important to avoid risk of injury. Do not forfeit any opportunity to escape from arm locks, but surrender when further resistance will lead to injury. Arm locks usually hurt, but this varies from person to person, so proper training about the elbow's vulnerability to dislocation helps prevent injury.

The most important safety rule for arm locks is to release pressure immediately when the opponent signals defeat by tapping. You should have sufficient control over your opponent to recognize when the lock takes effect, so you can release pressure before injury even if *uke* does not tap. Once an arm is extended to the limit of its range of motion, *uke's* ability to resist is greatly diminished so you must make sure that your application of pressure is careful and measured.

Below: The most powerful arm bars use your entire body to apply pressure to the joint.

UDE GARAMI (entangled arm lock)

This popular bent-arm lock can be applied from many different positions—standing, from a pin, or from underneath *uke*. The angle of the arm you are attacking must be bent, with the hand pointing either up above *uke*'s head, or down towards *uke*'s feet. In different variations of this technique you may push *uke*'s hand away from you, pull *uke*'s elbow towards you, bring *uke*'s hand in towards *uke*'s shoulder, or a combination of movements.

This arm lock can be used to apply pressure on *uke*'s shoulder, potentially separating or dislocating it. This is useful when standing to force *uke* to the ground, or when on the ground to roll *uke* over. With additional study and greater skill, the pressure can be applied on the elbow, and you will be able to dislocate it if necessary.

Key points:

- Gain control over *uke*'s movement, and immobilize *uke*'s shoulder.
- Grab *uke*'s wrist so the back of your hand is towards you, and the thumb side of your hand is towards the elbow you are attacking.
- Place your other forearm behind *uke*'s elbow, then grab your own wrist. The back of your hand should be facing towards you.
- Maintain pressure on the elbow and slide it towards *uke*'s waist.

Variation

Variation

Variation

Variation

UDE HISHIGI JUJI GATAME (cross arm lock)

Commonly called *juji gatame*, this cross arm lock gets its name from your position across your opponent's body. One of the most effective arm locks in judo, it is consistently the number-one winning arm lock used in international judo competition. It is a specialty of the 1981 World Champion, Neil Adams, of the United Kingdom. It is equally effective in high-level competition and in self-defense, and is included in many modern and traditional *jujutsu* systems. It is particularly powerful because you use your entire body, including the strength of the legs and hips, to control *uke* and apply tremendous pressure to the straightened arm. For this reason it can be used easily against larger or stronger opponents.

Key points:

- Control *uke*'s wrist with your hands so the little finger side of *uke*'s hand is against your chest.
- Control *uke*'s shoulder by squeezing your knees together, and control *uke*'s body with your legs.
- Keep *uke*'s elbow around your hips or abdomen, and bridge your body (raise the hips) if necessary to apply pressure on the elbow.

Application following a throw

Variation: *gyaku juji gatame*

UDE HISHIGI UDE GATAME (straight arm lock)

Ude gatame is a simple, direct arm lock that can be applied while standing to bring an opponent down, or on the ground to force submission. Although it looks simple, exact placement and body control are needed to make it effective against a resisting opponent.

Key points:

- Use your head to trap *uke*'s hand or wrist on your shoulder.
- Cup both hands on the point of the elbow.
- Focussing the pressure on the little-finger side of your hands, force *uke*'s straightened arm into hyperextension.

UDE HISHIGI HIZA GATAME (knee arm lock)

Hiza gatame is used in the *Katame no Kata* by forcing *uke* face down on the ground. By straightening your opponent's arm and using your knee to apply downward pressure on the elbow you can prevent escape and make *uke* submit.

Key points:

- Hold *uke*'s wrist with your hands and stretch *uke*'s arm straight.
- Put your foot on *uke*'s hip for leverage and control.
- Place your knee on top of *uke*'s elbow and push down.

Variation

UDE HISHIGI WAKI GATAME (armpit arm lock)

Waki gatame is a strong lock that uses your own body weight against *uke*'s elbow joint. When attempting this from a standing position, be careful to give your opponent an opportunity to tap—fast and forceful execution can result in injury. It is useful for self-defense, and can be effective against an opponent who is stiff-arming you to keep you away.

Key points:
- With both hands, grip *uke*'s wrist so your thumbs are close to *uke*'s hand.
- Place your right elbow over *uke*'s arm so your shoulder is just above *uke*'s elbow joint.
- Gain control of *uke*'s shoulder by forcing it to the ground, then lean on the elbow and lift *uke*'s hand to apply pressure on the elbow.

Variation: *gyaku waki gatame*

UDE HISHIGI HARA GATAME (stomach arm lock)

Hara is the place in your abdomen where your center of gravity is when you are upright. Traditionally considered in Eastern thought to be the seat of the soul and the center of *ki*, or life force, it is located just below your navel. This part of your body is used directly against the elbow joint in *hara gatame*.

Key points:
- Control *uke*'s wrist so *uke*'s thumb points away from you.
- Control *uke*'s shoulder with your hand across the throat or by grabbing the lapel.
- Thrust your hips directly into the extended elbow joint while pulling *uke*'s wrist and head back.

UDE HISHIGI ASHI GATAME (leg arm lock)

Ashi gatame is performed when you are beside *uke*, who is either face down on the ground or face up. Any arm lock using your feet is called *ashi gatame*, so there are many variations.

Key points:
- Apply *kesa gatame* (page 120).
- When *uke* frees the arm, straighten it over your thigh.
- Apply downward pressure on the wrist with your foot.

UDE HISHIGI TE GATAME (hand arm lock)

As the name implies, *te gatame* uses only your hands to effect the extension of the arm.

Key points:

- Immediately after throwing *uke*, control the wrist with one hand.
- With the other hand reach under *uke*'s arm and across *uke*'s throat to grip the far lapel, fingers inside, anchoring it and preventing *uke* from turning.
- Draw *uke*'s arm across your own arm as you straighten your own arm into the elbow.

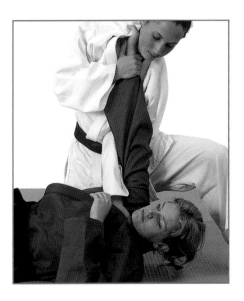

UDE HISHIGI SANKAKU GATAME
(triangle arm lock)

This is very similar to the position of the choking technique, *sankaku jime* (page 137), except in this case you use the trapped arm to apply an arm bar. Like the choke, it can be applied from many different positions.

Key points:

- Trap *uke*'s head and one arm between your legs.
- Lock your legs together with one foot behind your other knee.
- Straighten *uke*'s arm and pull *uke*'s wrist into your chest as you thrust your hips forward into *uke*'s elbow.

Application from the bottom

Appendices

Appendix 1:

TECHNIQUES RECOGNIZED BY THE KODOKAN

Dai Ikkyo (1st group)

Deashi harai

Hiza guruma

Sasae tsurikomi ashi

Uki goshi

Osoto gari

O goshi

Ouchi gari

Seoi nage

Dai Nikyo (2nd group)

Kosoto gari

Kouchi gari

Koshi guruma

Tsurikomi goshi

Okuri ashi harai

Tai otoshi

Harai goshi

Uchi mata

Sankyo (3rd group)

Kosoto gake

Tsuri goshi

Yoko otoshi

Ashi guruma

Hane goshi

Harai tsurikomi ashi

Tomoe nage

Kata guruma

Yonkyo (4th group)

Sumi gaeshi

Tani otoshi

Hane makikomi

Sukui nage

Utsuri goshi

O guruma

Soto makikomi

Uki otoshi

Gokyo (5th group)

Osoto guruma

Uki waza

Yoko wakare

Yoko guruma

Ushiro goshi

Ura nage

Sumi otoshi

Yoko gake

Habukareta waza

(preserved techniques
from 1895 gokyo)

Obi otoshi

Seoi otoshi

Yama arashi

Osoto otoshi

Daki wakare

Hikikomi gaeshi

Tawara gaeshi

Shinmeisho no waza

(newly accepted techniques)

Morote gari

Kibisu gaeshi

Daki age

Kouchi gaeshi

Osoto gaeshi

Uchi Mata gaeshi

Kani basami

Kawazu gake

Uchi mata makikomi

Ippon seoi nage

Kuchiki taoshi

Uchi mata sukashi

Tsubame gaeshi

Ouchi gaeshi

Harai goshi gaeshi

Hane goshi gaeshi

Osoto maki komi

Harai maki komi

Sode tsurikomi goshi

Appendix 2:

TECHNIQUES RECOGNIZED BY THE INTERNATIONAL JUDO FEDERATION

Te waza

Ippon seoi nage

Kata guruma

Kibisu gaeshi

Kouchi gaeshi

Kuchiki taoshi

Morote gari

Obi otoshi

Obi tori gaeshi

Seoi nage

Seoi otoshi

Sukui nage

Sumi otoshi

Tai otoshi

Uchi mata sukashi

Uki otoshi

Yama arashi

Koshi waza

Hane goshi

Harai goshi

Koshi guruma

O goshi

Sode tsurikomi goshi

Tsuri goshi

Tsurikomi goshi

Uki goshi

Ushiro goshi

Utsuri goshi

Ma sutemi waza

Hikikomi gaeshi

Sumi gaeshi

Tawara gaeshi

Tomoe nage

Ura nage

Uchi mata makikomi

Ashi waza

Ashi guruma

Deashi harai

Hane goshi gaeshi

Harai goshi gaeshi

Harai tsurikomi ashi

Hiza guruma

Kosoto gake

Kosoto gari

Kouchi gari

O guruma

Okuriashi harai

Osoto gari

Osoto gaeshi

Osoto guruma

Osoto otoshi

Ouchi gaeshi

Yoko sutemi waza

Yoko wakare

Yoko otoshi

Yoko guruma

Yoko gake

Uki waza

Kouchi makikomi

Daki wakare

Hane makikomi

Harai makikomi

Osoto makikomi

Soto makikomi

Tani otoshi

Uchi makikomi

Uchi mata makikomi

Shime waza

Gyaku juji jime

Hadaka jime

Kataha jime

Kata juji jime

Kata te jime

Nami juji jime

Okuri eri jime

Ryo te jime

Sankaku jime

Sode guruma jime

Tsukkomi jime

Kinshi waza

Ashi garami

Do jime

Kani basami

Kawazu gake

Appendix 3:

COMBINATION AND COUNTER TECHNIQUES
(*KAESHI* AND *RENRAKU WAZA*)

This table gives you an idea of how to combine various throws into effective integrated attack systems. Throwing techniques are listed in alphabetical order by the Japanese name, followed by the throws that can be used in combination to set up your opponent for the first throw, or to attack an opponent who has escaped your first attempt at a throw. The last column gives examples of what throws to use to counter an attack by your opponent.

The appropriate follow-up technique depends largely on exactly how your opponent attempts to escape your first throw. The appropriate counter also depends on exploiting the weakness in your opponent's technique, so not every counter will work the same against different attackers. In some cases, a right-sided attack is followed by a left-sided combination or counter. While this list is comprehensive, many other *kaeshi waza* and *renraku waza* can be used to throw your opponent.

THROWING TECHNIQUE	SET-UP ATTACK	FOLLOW-UP ATTACK	COUNTERATTACK
Ashi guruma Foot wheel	*Deashi harai* *Okuriashi harai* *Osoto gari*	*Osoto gari* *Tai otoshi*	*Nidan kosoto gari* *Te guruma* *Sukui nage*
Deashi harai Advancing foot sweep	*Ouchi gari*	*Tai otoshi* *Morote seoi nage*	*Tsubame gaeshi* *Harai goshi*
Hane goshi Spring hip throw	*Deashi harai* *Okuriashi harai* *Kouchi gari*	*Ouchi gari* *Kouchi gari* *Hane makikomi*	*Hane goshi gaeshi* *Ushiro goshi* *Utsuri goshi* *Tani otoshi* *Yoko guruma*
Harai goshi Sweeping hip throw	*Deashi harai* *Kouchi gari* *Osoto gari*	*Osoto gari* *Harai makikomi* *Ashi guruma*	*Ushiro goshi* *Te guruma* *Utsuri goshi* *Ura nage* *Harai goshi gaeshi*
Hiza guruma Knee wheel	*Osoto gari* *Deashi harai*	*Osoto gari* *Kosoto gari* *Deashi harai* *Harai goshi*	*Kouchi gari* *Kuchiki taoshi* *Ouchi gari*
Kani basami Flying scissors	*Harai goshi* *O guruma*	*Ne waza*	*Tani otoshi* *Nidan kosoto gari*
Koshi guruma Hip wheel	*Ouchi gari* *Harai goshi*	*Osoto gari* *Ouchi gari* *Soto makikomi*	*Ushiro goshi* *Utsuri goshi* *Tani otoshi*
Kosoto gake Small outside hook	*Okuriashi harai* *Deashi harai*	*Kosoto gari* *Tai otoshi* *Ouchi gari*	*Uchi mata* *Ouchi gari*

THROWING TECHNIQUE	SET-UP ATTACK	FOLLOW-UP ATTACK	COUNTERATTACK
Kosoto gari Small outside reap	Hiza guruma Ouchi gari Uki goshi	Sasae tsurikomi ashi Kibisu gaeshi Nidan kosoto gari Harai goshi Tai otoshi	Uchi mata Kani basami Ouchi gari
Kouchi gari Small inner reap	Ouchi gari Uchi mata Ippon seoi nage Tai otoshi	Ouchi gari Seoi nage Kuchiki taoshi Harai tsurikomi ashi	Hiza guruma Nidan kosoto gari Kouchi gaeshi Tani otoshi Tomoe nage
Kouchi makikomi Small inner wraparound	Ouchi gari Ippon seoi nage Kouchi gari	Ouchi gari Ippon seoi nage	Hiza guruma Sumi gaeshi Kouchi gaeshi
Morote gari Two hand reap	Kosoto gari Seoi nage	Kouchi makikomi Ouchi gari	Tawara gaeshi Sumi gaeshi Hikikomi gaeshi Uchi mata
Nidan kosoto gari Double outside reap	Osoto gari Kosoto gari	Tani otoshi	Uchi mata Ouchi gari
O goshi Large hip throw	Ouchi gari Kouchi gari Uki goshi	Ouchi gari Kouchi gari Harai goshi	Ushiro goshi Utsuri goshi Yoko guruma Tani otoshi
O guruma Large wheel	Deashi harai	Kani basami Ashi guruma	Ushiro goshi Utsuri goshi Tani otoshi
Okuriashi harai Sliding foot sweep	Sasae tsurikomi ashi	Tai Otoshi Harai Goshi Seoi Otoshi Seoi Nage	Tsubame Gaeshi Harai Goshi Kouchi Gari
Osoto gari Large outer reap	Harai goshi Seoi nage Ashi guruma	Nidan kosoto gari Sasae tsurikomi ashi Harai goshi Hiza guruma Osoto makikomi Osoto otoshi Uchi mata	Osoto gaeshi Harai goshi Osoto makikomi Ura nage Sukui nage
Ouchi gari Large inner reap	Kouchi gari Tai otoshi Tsuri goshi Hane goshi Osoto gari	Uchi mata Tai otoshi Osoto gari Kouchi gari	Ouchi gaeshi Nidan kosoto gari Ippon seoi nage Tomoe nage

THROWING TECHNIQUE	SET-UP ATTACK	FOLLOW-UP ATTACK	COUNTERATTACK
Sasae tsurikomi ashi Propping lifting pulling throw	Osoto gari	Harai goshi Osoto gari	Kouchi gari Ouchi gari Osoto gari
Seoi nage Shoulder throw	Kouchi gari Osoto gari	Kouchi gari Osoto gari Sukui nage Uchi makikomi Seoi otoshi	Ushiro goshi Sukui nage Utsuri goshi Tani otoshi Okuri eri jime
Seoi otoshi Shoulder drop	Deashi harai Ouchi gari	Ouchi gari Osoto gari Kibisu gaeshi	Kosoto gake Okuri eri jime
Sode tsurikomi goshi Sleeve lifting pulling hip	Ouchi gari Osoto gari	Ouchi gari Osoto gari	Ushiro goshi Sukui nage Tani otoshi
Sumi gaeshi Corner reversal	Deashi harai Ouchi gari	Ouchi gari Juji gatame	Ouchi gari Kuchiki taoshi
Tai otoshi Body drop	Deashi harai Ouchi gari Tai otoshi	Tai otoshi Ouchi gari Yoko tomoe nage Kouchi gari	Kosoto gake Yoko guruma
Tani otoshi Valley drop	Kosoto gari Harai goshi	Nidan kosoto gari	Uchi mata Ouchi gari
Tomoe nage Circular throw	Deashi harai Tai otoshi	Juji gatame	Ouchi gari Kouchi gari Kuchiki taoshi
Tsuri goshi Lifting hip	Kouchi gari Ouchi gari	Kouchi gari Ouchi gari Harai goshi	Ushiro goshi Sukui nage Utsuri goshi O goshi Tani otoshi Ura nage
Tsurikomi goshi Lifting pulling hip	Kouchi gari Ouchi gari	Kouchi gari Ouchi gari	Ushiro goshi Sukui nage Utsuri goshi Tani otoshi
Uchi mata Inner thigh throw	Kouchi gari Ouchi gari Deashi harai Osoto gari	Tai otoshi Kouchi gari Ouchi gari Uchi mata makikomi	Uchi mata gaeshi Uchi mata sukashi Te guruma Ura nage

Appendix 4: FORMS (*KATA*)

NAGE NO KATA (THROWING FORMS)

Te waza (hand techniques)
- *Uki otoshi*
- *Seoi nage*
- *Kata guruma*

Koshi waza (hip techniques)
- *Uki goshi*
- *Harai goshi*
- *Tsurikomi goshi*

Ashi waza (foot/leg techniques)
- *Okuri ashi harai*
- *Sasae tsurikomi ashi*
- *Uchi mata*

Ma sutemi waza (rear sacrifice techniques)
- *Tomoe nage*
- *Ura nage*
- *Sumi gaeshi*

Yoko sutemi waza (side sacrifice techniques)
- *Yoko gake*
- *Yoko guruma*
- *Uki waza*

KATAME NO KATA (GRAPPLING FORMS)

Osaekomi waza (pinning techniques)
- *Kesa gatame*
- *Kata gatame*
- *Kamishiho gatame*
- *Yokoshiho gatame*
- *Kuzure kamishiho gatame*

Shime waza (choking techniques)
- *Kata juji jime*
- *Hadaka jime*
- *Okuri eri jime*
- *Kataha jime*
- *Gyaku juji jime*

Kansetsu waza (joint locking techniques)
- *Ude garami*
- *Ude hishigi juji gatame*
- *Ude hishigi ude gatame*
- *Ude hishigi hiza gatame*
- *Ashi garami*

Appendix 5: TOURNAMENT RULES AND SCORING

Start of a contest

After the contestants have bowed and stepped forward, the referee announces *hajime* (begin) to start the contest.

Scoring a contest
- *Ippon* (full point)
- *Waza ari* (almost *ippon* or half point)
- *Yuko* (almost *waza ari*)
- *Koka* (almost *yuko*)

Penalties
- *Hansoku make* (very serious violation; disqualification)
- *Shido* (minor violation; *koka* awarded to opponent the first time; increasing score each time there is another *shido*)

Objective

In judo competition the objective is to score an *ippon* (one full point). Once such a score is obtained the competition ends. An *ippon* can be scored by one of the following methods:

- Executing a skillful throwing technique that results in a contestant being thrown, largely on the back, with considerable force or speed.
- Maintaining control of opponent in a pin for 25 seconds.
- One contestant cannot continue and gives up.
- One contestant is disqualified for violating the rules (*hansoku make*).
- Applying an effective arm lock or stranglehold (this does not usually apply to children).

- Earning two *waza ari* (half points). A *waza ari* can be earned by: (1) a throwing technique that is not quite an *ippon* (e.g. the opponent lands only partly on the back, or with less force than required for *ippon*); (2) holding a contestant in a pin for at least 20 seconds; or (3) when the opponent violates the rules (*shido*) three times.

If time runs out with neither contestant scoring an *ippon*, the referee will award the win to the contestant with the next highest score. For example, a contestant with one *yuko* would win against an opponent who scored four *kokas*. In the event of an *ied* score at the end of the match time, a Golden Score period begins and contestants continue to fight. The first one to earn any score wins.

Scoreboards

Because it is always the highest quality score that wins in judo, the scoreboard is laid out left to right to show the scores in a numerical fashion. Looked at in this way, the score in the illustration is 31 to 100: white's single *waza ari* beats the lesser quality of blue's three *yukos* and one *koka*. An *ippon* score is not shown on the scoreboard because there can only be one *ippon*—and it ends the match.

Waza Ari	Yuko	Koka	Waza Ari	Yuko	Koka
0	3	1	1	0	0

Referee signals

Ippon (full point): Opponent is thrown on the back with force, held under control in a pin on the mat for 25 seconds, or an effective choke or arm lock is applied.

Waza ari (near *ippon*): Throw is not completely successful, or opponent is held under control in a pin for at least 20 seconds.

Yuko (almost *waza ari*): Throw is partially successful, or opponent is held under control in a pin for 15 to 20 seconds.

Koka (almost *yuko*): Throw is minimally successful, so the opponent's hip, shoulder or side touches the mat, or opponent is held under control in a pin for at least 10 seconds.

Osaekomi (mat hold begins): Opponent is held under control on his or her back and the time starts.

Mate (stop): The match is temporarily stopped and the time clock pauses.

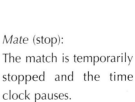

Appendix 6:

COMPETITION PENALTIES AND PROHIBITED ACTS

Prohibited acts are divided into slight infringements (*shido*) and grave infringements (*hansoku make*). The referee awards a penalty of *shido* or *hansoku make*, depending on the seriousness of the infringement. The awarding of a second or subsequent *shido* automatically reflects on the opponent's technical score. The previous score corresponding to the earlier penalty is removed and the next highest score is recorded immediately. The awarding of a direct *hansoku make* means the contestant is disqualified and excluded from the tournament, and the contest ends.

Shido (slight infringements)

1. Intentionally avoiding taking *kumikata* in order to prevent action in the contest.

2. Adopting in a standing position, after *kumikata*, an excessively defensive posture (generally more than five seconds).

3. Making an action designed to give the impression of an attack but clearly showing there was no intent to throw the opponent (false attack).

4. Standing with both feet completely within the danger zone unless beginning or executing an attack, countering the opponent's attack or defending against the opponent's attack (generally more than five seconds).

5. In a standing position, continually holding the opponent's sleeve end(s) for a defensive purpose (generally more than five seconds) or grasping by "screwing up" the sleeve end(s).

6. In a standing position, continually keeping the opponent's fingers of one or both hands interlocked, in order to prevent action in the contest (generally more than five seconds).

7. Intentionally disarranging one's own *judogi* or untying or retying the belt or trousers without the referee's permission.

8. Pulling the opponent down in order to start *ne waza* unless in accordance with Article 16 (which generally requires a throw or other skillful technique rather than simply pulling your opponent to the ground).

9. Inserting a finger or fingers inside the opponent's sleeve or bottom of his trousers.

10. In a standing position, taking any grip other than a 'normal' grip without attacking (generally more than five seconds). 'Normal' *kumikata* is taking hold of the right side of the opponent's *judogi* with the left hand, or the left side of the opponent's *judogi* with the right hand—be it the sleeve, collar, chest area, top of the shoulder, or back, and always above the belt. A contestant should not be penalized for holding with an abnormal grip if this is caused by the opponent ducking his head beneath the holder's arm. However, if a contestant is continually ducking this way, the referee should consider whether he is adopting an "excessively defensive posture" (see 2 above). If a contestant continues to take an abnormal *kumikata*, the time allowed may be progressively reduced, or he may incur a "direct penalty" of *shido*. Hooking one leg between the opponent's legs unless simultaneously attempting a throwing technique is not considered normal *kumikata* and the contestant must attack within five seconds or the contestant will be penalized with *shido*.

11. In a standing position, before or after *kumikata* has been established, not making any attacking moves. "Non-combativity" is considered to exist when in general there have been no attacking actions on the part of one or both contestants for approximately 25 seconds. Non-combativity should not be awarded when there are no attacking actions if the referee considers that the contestant is genuinely looking for the opportunity to attack.

12. Holding the opponent's sleeve end(s) between the thumb and the fingers ("pistol" grip).

13. Holding the opponent's sleeve end(s) by folding it over ("pocket" grip).

14. From a standing position, taking hold of the opponent's foot/feet, leg(s), or trouser leg(s) with the hand(s), unless simultaneously attempting a throwing technique.

15. Encircling the end of the belt or jacket around any part of the opponent's body. This means the belt or jacket must completely encircle the body part. Using the belt or jacket as an anchor for a grip (without encircling), e.g. to trap the opponent's arm, should not be penalized.

16. Taking the *judogi* in the mouth (either his own or his opponent's *judogi*).

17. Putting a hand, arm, foot, or leg directly on the opponent's face. The face means the area within the line bordered by the forehead, the front of the ears and the jaw line.

18. Putting a foot or leg in opponent's belt, collar, or lapel.

19. Applying *shime waza* using the bottom of the jacket or belt, or using only the fingers.

20. Going outside the contest area or intentionally forcing the opponent to go outside the contest area, either in standing position or in *ne waza*.

21. Applying leg scissors to the opponent's trunk (*dojime*), neck, or head (scissor with crossed feet, while stretching out the legs).

22. Kicking the opponent's hand or arm with the knee or foot to make him release his grip, or kicking the opponent's leg or ankle without applying any technique.

23. Bending back the opponent's finger(s) in order to break a grip.

Hansoku make (grave infringements)

24. Applying *kawazu gake* (throwing the opponent by winding one leg around the opponent's leg, while facing more or less in the same direction as the opponent and falling backwards onto him). Even if the thrower twists/turns during the throwing action, this should still be considered *kawazu gake* and be penalized. Techniques such as *osoto gari*, *ouchi gari*, and *uchi mata*, where the foot/leg is entwined with opponent's leg, are permitted and should be scored.

25. Applying *kansetsu waza* anywhere other than to the elbow joint.

26. Lifting an opponent lying on the *tatami* off the *tatami* and driving him back onto the *tatami*.

27. Reaping the opponent's supporting leg from the inside when the opponent is applying a technique such as *harai goshi*, etc.

28. Disregarding the referee's instructions.

29. Making unnecessary calls, remarks, or gestures derogatory to the opponent or referee during contest.

30. Taking any action that may endanger or injure the opponent (especially the opponent's neck or spinal vertebrae) or that is against the spirit of judo.

31. Falling directly to the *tatami* while applying or attempting to apply techniques such as *ude hishigi waki gatame*. Attempting such throws as *harai goshi*, *uchi mata*, etc., with only one hand gripping the opponent's lapel from a position resembling *ude hishigi waki gatame* (in which the wrist of the opponent is trapped beneath the thrower's armpit) and deliberately falling face down onto the *tatami* is likely to cause injury and will be penalized. No intent to throw an opponent cleanly onto his back is a dangerous action and will be treated in the same way as *ude hishigi waki gatame*.

32. Diving head first onto the *tatami* by bending forward and downward while performing or attempting to perform techniques such as *uchi mata*, *harai goshi*, etc., or falling directly backwards while performing or attempting to perform techniques such as *kata guruma*, whether standing or kneeling.

33. Intentionally falling backwards when the opponent is clinging to your back and when either contestant has control of the other's movement.

34. Wearing a hard or metallic object (covered or not).

Referees and judges are authorized to award penalties according to the "intent" or situation and in the best interest of the sport. If the referee decides to penalize the contestant(s)—except in the case of *sono mama* in *ne waza*—he temporarily stops the contest by announcing *mate*, returns the contestants to their starting positions and announces the penalty while pointing to the contestant(s) who committed the prohibited act.

Where both contestants infringe the rules at the same time, each should be awarded a penalty according to the seriousness of the infringement. Where both contestants have been given three *shidos* and each subsequently receives a further penalty, both should be declared *hansoku make*.

On the scoreboard, the repeated *shido* will be accumulated and converted to the opponent's technical score:
  1 *shido* = a *koka* to the opponent
  2 *shidos* = a *yuko* to the opponent
  3 *shidos* = a *waza ari* to the opponent
  4 *shidos* = *hansoku make* = *ippon* to the opponent

ONLINE RESOURCES

These web sites are considered to be the most reliable and current sources of information about judo.

www.IJF.org

The International Judo Federation's site has details on international competition and sport judo, including contacts for national judo organizations in each country.

www.JudoInfo.com

Comprehensive source of information about all aspects of judo, including contacts for judo classes around the world, online judo lessons, articles, links and videos/animations of judo techniques.

www.JudoForum.com

Provides the opportunity to read or participate in discussion of current events in the world of judo, and other topics of interest, e.g. advice, training tips, philosophy, and gear.

www.BestJudo.com

The most complete listing of judo books online, with a review and extensive information about each.

www.twoj.org

The site of *The World of Judo*, the official magazine of the British Judo Association, includes lots of judo tournament photographs.

You can also contact:
International Judo Federation Headquarters
33rd FL Doosan Tower, 18-12, Ulchi-Ro 6-Ka, Chung-Ku, Seoul, Korea 100-300
Tel: +82 2 3398-1017
Fax: +82 2 3398-1020
E-mail: info@ijf.org

Glossary

Aiyotsu	Same grip used by both persons, either right or left
Ashi	Foot, leg
Ashi waza	Foot techniques
Atemi waza	Striking techniques
Ayumi ashi	Ordinary pattern of walking
Batsugun	Instant promotion
Budo	Martial arts (the way of war)
Bushido	Way of the warrior
Dan	Black belt rank
Debana	Instant of opportunity to break balance as opponent initiates a motion
Dojo	School or training hall for studying the way
Eri	Collar, lapel
Fudoshin	Immovable spirit
Fusegi	Escapes
Fusen gachi	Win by default
Go no sen	Reactive initiative; attacking in response to an attack
Goshin jutsu waza	Self-defense techniques
Hajime	Begin
Hando no kuzushi	Unbalancing by reaction
Hansokumake	Most serious penalty, disqualification
Hantei	Referee call for judge's decision
Happo no kuzushi	Breaking balance in eight directions
Hara	Stomach
Hidari	Left
Hiji	Elbow
Hiki wake	No decision, tie or draw
Hikidashi	Pulling out
Hikite	Pulling hand, usually the hand gripping a sleeve
Hiza	Knee
Ippon	One point in competition
Jigotai	Defensive posture
Jikan	Referee call to stop the clock
Jime	Strangle or choke
Jita kyoei	Principle of mutual prosperity
Joseki	Place of honor, upper seat
Judo	Gentle or flexible way
Judo ichidai	Spending life in diligent pursuit of judo
Judogi	Judo practice uniform
Judoka	One who studies judo
Ju no kata	Forms of gentleness
Ju no ri	Principle of flexibility or yielding
Jujutsu	Gentle art
Kaeshi waza	Counter techniques
Kake	Completion or execution of technique
Kansetsu waza	Joint locking techniques
Kappo (katsu)	Resuscitation techniques
Kata	Forms; also shoulder
Katame no Kata	Forms of grappling
Kenka yotsu	Opposite grips used by each person, one right/one left
Ki	Spirit, life force

Kiai	To gather spirit with a shout	Shintai	Moving forward, sideways, and backward
Kihon	Basics, fundamentals	Shisei	Posture
Kime no kata	Forms of decision	Shizentai	Natural posture
Kinshi waza	Techniques prohibited in competition	Shomen	Front of the training hall
Ki o tsuke	Attention	Sode	Sleeve
Kodansha	High ranking judoka, 5th dan and above	Soke	Founder of a martial art or ryu
		Sono mama	Stop action; referee command to freeze
Kodokan	Judo institute in Tokyo where judo was founded	Sore made	Finished, time is up
Kogeki seyo	Order for judoka to attack	Sute geiko	Randori practice against a higher-level judoka
Koka	Score less than a yuko		
Koshi	Hip	Sutemi waza	Sacrifice techniques
Koshi waza	Hip techniques	Tachi waza	Standing techniques
Kubi	Neck	Tai sabaki	Body control, turning
Kumikata	Gripping methods	Tatami	Mat
Kuzure	Modified or broken hold	Te	Hand, arm
Kuzushi	Unbalancing the opponent	Te waza	Hand techniques
Kyoshi	Instructor	Tekubi	Wrist
Kyu	Student rank	Tobikomi	Jumping in
Maai	Space or engagement distance	Tokui waza	Favorite or best technique
Mae	Forward, front	Tori	Person performing a technique
Mae ukemi	Falling forward	Tsugi ashi	Walking by bringing one foot up to another
Ma sutemi waza	Rear sacrifice throws		
Mawarikomi	Spinning in for a throw	Tsukuri	Entry into a technique, positioning
Mate	Stop	Tsurite	Lifting hand
Migi	Right	Uchikomi	Repeated practice without completion
Mizu no kokoro	Mind like water		
Mudansha	Students below black belt rank	Ude	Arm
Mune	Chest	Uke	Person receiving the technique
Nage	Throw	Ukemi	Break-fall techniques
Nage no Kata	Forms of throwing	Ushiro	Backward, rear
Nagekomi	Repetitive throwing practice	Ushiro sabaki	Back movement control
Nage waza	Throwing techniques	Ushiro ukemi	Falling backward
Ne waza	Techniques on the ground	Waki	Armpit
Obi	Judo belt	Waza	Technique
Okuden	Secret teachings	Waza ari	Near ippon or half point
Osaekomi	Pin, referee call to begin timing	Waza ari awasete ippon	Two waza ari for the win
Osaekomi waza	Pinning techniques		
Osaekomi toketa	Escape, stop timing of hold	Yakusoku renshu (or geiko)	Prearranged form of repetitive practice
Randori	Free practice		
Randori no kata	Forms of free practice techniques (Nage no Kata and Katame no Kata)	Yoko	Side
		Yoko kaiten ukemi	Sideways rolling break-fall
Randori waza	Techniques for free practice	Yoko sutemi waza	Side sacrifice throws
Rei	Bow	Yoko ukemi	Falling sideways
Reiho	Forms of respect, manners, etiquette	Yoshi	Resume action, referee command to continue
Renraku waza	Combination techniques		
Ritsurei	Standing bow	Yubi	Finger
Seika tanden	A point in the abdomen that is the center of gravity	Yudansha	Person who has earned black belt
		Yudanshakai	Black belt association
Seiryoku zenyo	Principle of maximum efficiency	Yuko	Score less than a waza ari
Seiza	Formal kneeling posture	Yusei gachi	Win by judge's decision
Sen	Attack initiative	Zanshin	Awareness
Sensei	Teacher, instructor	Zarei	Kneeling bow
Shiai	Contest	Zenpo kaiten ukemi	Forward rolling break-fall
Shiaijo	Competition area	Zubon	Pants
Shido	Penalty, equal to koka score		
Shihan	Title for a model teacher, teacher who sets the standard		
Shinpan	Referee		
Shime waza	Choking or strangling techniques		

Index

ACKNOWLEDGMENTS

The lessons shared in this book are gleaned from many years of help provided by various teachers, training partners, competitors, students, and visitors to JudoInfo.com, who all gave part of themselves. I would like to thank my wife Bernadette for her unfailing faith and encouragement. Thanks also to Ben Holmes, Jerrod Wilson and Wolfgang Doffek for their invaluable advice. Alex Butcher (6th Dan), Ian Geustyn (5th Dan), Jessica Butcher (2nd Dan), Alistair Hill, Madré Rinquest, Laura Schwormstedt, and Denton Smith (1st Dans) gave of their time to assist; their expertise is reflected in the high quality of the demonstration photographs. Further thanks to Hatashita International at HatashitaInternational.com for their support of judo, and for providing the Mizuno Yawara *judogi* used by the author.